DATE DUE

MAY 1 0

WILLIAM GRAHAM SUMNER (1840-1910) was a pioneer American sociologist and political economist who had a strong sense of the scholar's obligation to play a part in the formation of public opinion and policy. In lectures and essays published in the popular magazines he sought to disseminate an understanding of what he believed to be the social forces which had shaped the inherited structure of institutions and determined the forms and limits within which men must act.

Sumner was by no means a mere apologist for business enterprise. Rather, he was the champion of a rapidly vanishing middle class whose members he designated Forgotten Men. His loyalties centered upon an older and simpler order; and he anticipated with foreboding the rise of Big Business, Big Labor, and Big Government.

STOW PERSONS, currently Professor of History at the State University of Iowa, received his Ph.D. from Yale. He is the author of AMERICAN MINDS: A HISTORY OF IDEAS and editor of EVOLUTIONARY THOUGHT IN AMERICA.

Social Darwinism

Social Darwinism

Selected Essays
of William Graham Sumner, 1840-1910

With an Introduction by

STOW PERSONS

A SPECTRUM BOOK

Prentice-Hall, Inc.
Englewood Cliffs, N.J.

Acknowledgment

William Graham Sumner published numerous essays in a variety of popular journals with the object of influencing public opinion. After his death his colleague and disciple Albert Galloway Keller collected and edited these papers, together with several previously unpublished essays. Four volumes were published by the Yale University Press: *War and Other Essays* (1911), *Earth-Hunger and Other Essays* (1913), *The Challenge of Facts and Other Essays* (1914), and *The Forgotten Man and Other Essays* (1919). Permission by the Yale University Press to reprint certain of the essays is gratefully acknowledged.

Editors' Note

This book is a volume in the Classics in History Series of works in American history. The titles in the series have been chosen primarily from familiar works that are not easily accessible. In some cases we have also chosen to reprint once influential books that still have intrinsic interest or to create fresh collections of essays or letters that now exist only in scattered or expensive editions.

William E. Leuchtenburg

Bernard Wishy

Table of Contents

INTRODUCTION

Sumner's Science of Society

These essays written principally in the 1880's represent the
middle phase of William Graham Sumner's intellectual career,
when he was concerned with the practical application of his
sociological theories to the problems of economic and public
policy. He had earlier published studies in the history of American public finance; and he was to terminate his career as a
comprehensive cultural anthropologist.

Sumner was born in Paterson, New Jersey, in 1840 and died
in 1910. All of his work bears the impress of a firm and somber
personality. In an earlier age he would have epitomized the
Puritan divine or magistrate. In fact the precepts of the Puritan
ethic descended directly to him through his father, Thomas
Sumner, who had emigrated from England in 1836. The formative influence of the father, a self-educated machinist, stamped
the son with indelible qualities of stubborn independence, strict
integrity, and contempt for all forms of sentimentalism. Sumner
liked to observe that nature had condemned man to work, adding
grimly that it was work that killed. At an early age he read
Harriet Martineau's *Illustrations of Political Economy* where
he found the ethical precepts applied to economic situations
which were to remain his abiding criteria for social judgments.
The elements of his education were complete when he went to
Germany in the sixties to study for the ministry. There he
found in the professors of Biblical studies at Göttingen the

1

living models of dedication to the scientific ideal of disinterested pursuit of truth. Sumner would always think of himself as a scientist, preferring for his theories the term "science of society" rather than the more familiar "sociology." To his mind, the principal connotations of science were a materialistic concern with facts as opposed to ideas, and a hard-headed critique of the sentimental humanitarianism of the Gilded Age.

The budding interest in public affairs which Sumner had revealed as an undergraduate at Yale during the Civil War continued to grow during his theological studies and brief service in the ministry. While studying at Oxford in 1866 he had discussed with fellow students the possibilities of founding a science of society on historical principles, a question which he had regretfully concluded would have to be answered in the negative. The decisive event of his life occurred about 1870 when he read a series of articles by Herbert Spencer later to be published as *The Study of Sociology*. Here Sumner found key concepts and a general philosophic point of view which were to organize his thinking and furnish a framework for his life's work. He welcomed an opportunity to exchange the ministry for teaching, and in 1872 accepted an appointment as professor of political and social science at Yale.

The Spencerian world view that Sumner embroidered in his own fashion was a form of evolutionary naturalism. The erstwhile Episcopalian clergyman abandoned his Christian supernaturalism to confront a world of nature frankly acknowledged to be unreasoning and brutal. The best that man could hope for was partially to evade or soften natural processes by means of knowledge, disciplined methods, and technological arts. In spite of past achievements the odds were heavily against man's continuing success. It had been a combination of happy accidents that had thus far held his feet on the path of progress. Culture, as Sumner defined it, was the cultivation of any physical or psychological trait which helped in the struggle for existence; civilization was the collective term designating the complex of activities which distinguished man from beast. These definitions formed the core of a thoroughly materialistic interpretation of history and culture.

Sumner found men engaged in an unceasing struggle for existence with nature in order to extort from her the means of subsistence. Because nature was niggardly and did not normally provide enough for all, men also contended with one another in what Sumner called the competition of life for nature's limited resources. Wherever natural resources were plentiful and the number of men in competition was small their collision would be mild and free societies would flourish; otherwise it would be deadly, with slavery and other extreme forms of coercion the inevitable consequence. By failing to stress sufficiently this distinction between the struggle for existence against nature and the competition of life among men Sumner opened himself to the misconception that he was merely an apologist for laissez-faire individualism, when in fact this was only an incidental aspect of his social theory.

It is important to note that while in principle the competition of life occurred between individuals and expressed man's innate selfishness, in fact the competition always occurred between organized groups, the most primitive and ubiquitous of which was the family. Men everywhere had discovered that the struggle for existence with nature was carried on more effectively in groups than individually. Two contrasting codes of conduct thus resulted. Peace, cooperation, and friendliness within the group; hostility and competition with outsiders. Similar theories were commonly voiced by nineteenth-century socialists, and it is one of the paradoxes of Sumner that he managed to base his theory of individualism on the contrast.

The earliest and most enduring human groups had been formed for industrial purposes, a fact which underscored the strong materialistic and functional emphasis permeating Sumner's thinking. These industrial groups employed the technology which was the ultimate determinant of the character of the whole society. Economic, political, artistic, and ideological beliefs and practices had all been shaped by the relative effectiveness of the technology in converting nature's potential to human uses. Sumner used the word capital broadly to designate the technology, weapons, and economic resources with which both the struggle for existence and the competition of life were carried on. The accumulation and use of capital was of supreme importance, and those who controlled it were truly the masters of society.

The thorough-going materialism of Sumner's conception of the social structure with its technological base determined his analysis of social change. Progress occurred whenever fruitful technological innovations made possible more effective exploitation of nature's resources. Out of such innovations would flow subsequent adjustments in economic, social, and intellectual usages. Retrogression would occur, however, if social balances were disrupted: if, for instance, political action were taken to intervene in the industrial order. Sumner considered political action merely a refined form of arbitrary force. Directed against industrial processes it was simply dispossession. The motives for constructive industrial activity would then be weakened, and retrogression would follow. In Sumner's view, the major peril of the times lay in the tendency of democratic politics to intervene in economic affairs in the interests of reform.

Although Darwin was his hero among scientists, Sumner did not share the popular enthusiasm which found proof of social progress in Darwinian biological evolution. The scientific temper of mind as he understood it, far from supporting the current noisy and careless optimism, inculcated a critical and pessimistic outlook. It implied caution and doubt, as opposed to the popular gush, boasting, and rashness. The course of history was a patternless advance and retreat as men momentarily gained or lost in the struggle for existence. During the past four hundred years considerable advances had admittedly been made, thanks to the discovery of America and important technological innovations. But Sumner was no optimist, and he observed with foreboding certain tendencies which if unchecked promised to nullify recent advances and throw society back to more primitive conditions.

One of these ominous tendencies was the growth of ideology. As a materialist, Sumner made a basic distinction between the sequence of overt events that formed a causal chain flowing from human acts, and the purposes and intentions of the actors. The principles of social science were so imperfectly understood that there was rarely any connection between the purposes of men and the consequences of their acts. Ideological doctrines were nothing but vague and generalized statements of purpose, meaningless rhetoric that regimented and tyrannized over men. By manipulating ideological symbols the opinion-makers were able to dominate policy and undermine the possibilities of rational action. The utopianism of the modern political mentality seemed to Sumner to be symptomatic of the corruption of mind and character which had resulted from the prevalent fashion of forming social ideals without reference to actualities. Let men look hard at the facts and take such cautious steps as a sound social science would indicate to be appropriate.

Another cause for concern was what Sumner felt to be the impending conflict between democracy and plutocracy, or in other words, between the proletariat and the capitalistic middle class. While there were striking similarities between Sumner's analysis and that of the Marxists, the differences stemmed from the fact that while Sumner's sympathies lay with the middle class he anticipated a disastrous outcome regardless of which party emerged victorious. The peculiar defect of democratic majorities was their incompetence, to neutralize which the democratic politician was perforce obliged to fool the public with ideological blandishments in order to do surreptitiously what he knew must be done. On the other hand, plutocracy as Sumner defined it was a political order in which the ruling power was wealth. He regarded it as the most corrupt and decadent of all political systems. When democratic reformers in the name of economic equality brought the power of the state to bear upon economic affairs they created the conditions inviting plutocratic corruption of politics.

Sumner's notion of the role of politics in the social process was one of the less persuasive parts of his thinking. While he regarded industrial processes as fruitful and potentially progressive, "politics" was stultifying and at best merely negative. The only legitimate function of politics was to stabilize the existing industrial system and protect the rights of individuals in relation to it. He had persuaded himself that industry never resorted to politics unless, perhaps, in self defense; but whenever a democratic majority used political power to intervene in the industrial order the results were always injurious. His own practical experience in politics, as New Haven alderman and as investigator of Louisiana election returns, had been more in-structive than edifying, and his mistrust of the constructive po-tentialities of political action is to be attributed to practical as well as theoretical influences. The polemical quality of the pres-ent collection of essays owes less to any affection for businessmen than to contempt for politicians.

It is essential to distinguish the plutocrat from the legitimate capitalist, for whose social functions Sumner had the highest re-gard. A plutocrat was a capitalist who used the power of capital for political rather than industrial purposes, corrupting the political system while obtaining monopolies, franchises, and other special privileges. Popular reform parties were especially vulnerable to plutocratic corruption, and Sumner could only exhort his fellow citizens to reduce to a minimum the relations between state and industry. By the middle of the twentieth cen-tury such a denigration of politics would have the effect of mak-ing Sumner's entire system appear archaic. It should be recalled, however, that during the nineteenth century the distinction be-tween society and government that Tom Paine had so forcefully asserted was still an essential part of the American political mentality. Society was natural and beneficial, serving man's needs; government was merely the necessary check upon his evil propensities. Sumner refined and amplified this distinction by assigning to politics a peripheral place in the social structure. It had little to do with the fundamental struggle for existence with nature. He feared that instead of democratizing capitalism the reformers would succeed only in capitalizing democracy, which would mean the introduction of plutocracy. In his own day, Sumner felt that the power of capital was still chiefly social and industrial, and only in small measure political. To socialize industry would bring all of the power of capital into politics, with disastrous results. For when the power of capital and politics were combined the vices of either would be unchecked by the other.

The manifold symptoms of moral decay during the Gilded Age was an even more ominous portent for the future. Sumner was always a strict moralist, deploring the growing popularity of attempts to account for affairs exclusively in economic terms. Every situation, he insisted, had a moral dimension. The standard of living, for instance, was a moral product, a badge of "industrial honor," earned by hard work, self-denial, and disciplined application. If there was any respect in which modern society was superior to former societies it was found in the finer qualities of feeling that united the monogamous family. Sumner firmly believed that the regard for property was a product of family sentiment, and that the potential for capital accumulation was largely dependent upon the continuing stability of the family relationship.

A peculiar feature of Sumner's social evolutionism was the hinging of past and future upon relatively narrow and clearly specified elements in his own society. The independent, self-respecting and self-sufficing entrepreneurs and producers of nineteenth-century America were the fine flower of the historic process, and upon their welfare the future depended. Their origins endowed history with whatever significance it possessed, and their dubious prospects determined the essential pessimism with which Sumner faced the future. These independent citizens were the "forgotten men" who raised their families in dignity and peace, paid their bills and their taxes, and perpetuated the constructive values of the community. Amid the noisy clamor raised by reformers and demagogues on behalf of those alleged to be unable to support themselves the forgotten men were indeed forgotten.

Sumner's life-long aim as a scientist was to expand the domain of knowledge so that the consequences of acts would be better understood and a larger measure of social control be made possible. In the meantime, the essence of wisdom was to accept life as it was found, and to exercise reverent caution before acting willfully or "purposively." Paradoxically enough, where natural science meant experiment, manipulation, and change, Sumnerian social science meant acceptance of things as they were, and the imposition of strict limitations upon the legitimate scope of human activity. These principles disqualified Sumner as a prophet. "An economist or sociologist," he declared around the turn of the century, "who discusses socialism is like a physicist who discusses Jules Verne's novels. He does not prove his own breadth of mind; he proves that he does not understand the domain of his own vocation." Scarcely more than a generation after this pronouncement a large portion of the world's population was living under socialist governments, and the physicists had fairly outdone Jules Verne.

Far from being a conscious apologist for big business, Sumner developed a concept of democracy that was essentially Jeffersonian. The proper objects of politics were peace, order, and security. The only hope for the survival of democracy lay in the renunciation of social or industrial ends. Sumner yearned for a presumptive past, a past which perhaps never existed, when men had been left to their own devices. He warned of disaster in the intimate relationship of government and business. He regarded the separation of church and state as the most notable achievement of American democracy; and the principal item of unfinished business on the agenda was to be the separation of state and market. He persuaded himself that "if capital were excluded from all interest in state action, and thrown upon the laws of the market, there would remain only that power of capital which is rooted in the industrial and social order, which nothing can set aside or overcome." Surely this was a vision as utopian in its way as the vision of Edward Bellamy.

I

Sociology

Each of the sciences which, by giving to man greater knowledge of the laws of nature, has enabled him to cope more intelligently with the ills of life, has had to fight for its independence of metaphysics. We have still lectures on metaphysical biology in some of our colleges and in some of our public courses, but biology has substantially won its independence. Anthropology is more likely to give laws to metaphysics than to accept laws from that authority. Sociology, however, the latest of this series of sciences, is rather entering upon the struggle than emerging from it. Sociology threatens to withdraw an immense range of subjects of the first importance from the dominion of *a priori* speculation and arbitrary dogmatism, and the struggle will be severe in proportion to the dignity and importance of the subject. The struggle, however, is best carried forward indirectly, by simply defining the scope of sociology and by vindicating its position amongst the sciences, while leaving its relations to the other sciences and other pursuits of men to adjust themselves according to the facts. I know of nothing more amusing in these days than to see an old-fashioned metaphysician applying his tests to the results of scientific investigation, and screaming with rage because men of scientific training do not care whether the results satisfy those tests or not.

Sociology is the science of life in society. It investigates the forces which come into action wherever a human society exists.

It studies the structure and functions of the organs of human society, and its aim is to find out the laws in subordination to which human society takes its various forms and social institutions grow and change. Its practical utility consists in deriving the rules of right social living from the facts and laws which prevail by nature in the constitution and functions of society. It must, without doubt, come into collision with all other theories of right living which are founded on authority, tradition, arbitrary invention, or poetic imagination.

Sociology is perhaps the most complicated of all the sciences, yet there is no domain of human interest the details of which are treated ordinarily with greater facility. Various religions have various theories of social living, which they offer as authoritative and final. It has never, so far as I know, been asserted by anybody that a man of religious faith, in any religion, could not study sociology or recognize the existence of any such science; but it is incontestably plain that a man who accepts the dogmas about social living which are imposed by the authority of any religion must regard the subject of right social living as settled and closed, and he cannot enter on any investigation the first groundwork of which would be doubt of the authority which he recognizes as final. Hence social problems and social phenomena present no difficulty to him who has only to cite an authority or obey a prescription.

Then again the novelists set forth "views" about social matters. To write and read novels is perhaps the most royal road to teaching and learning which has ever been devised. The proceeding of the novelists is kaleidoscopic. They turn the same old bits of colored glass over and over again into new combinations. There is no limit, no sequence, no bond of consistency. The romance-writing social philosopher always proves his case, just as a man always wins who plays chess with himself.

Then again the utopians and socialists make easy work of the complicated phenomena with which sociology has to deal. These persons, vexed with the intricacies of social problems and revolting against the facts of the social order, take upon themselves the task of inventing a new and better world. They brush away all which troubles us men and create a world free from annoying limitations and conditions—in their imagination. In ancient times, and now in half-civilized countries, these persons have been founders of religions. Something of that type always lingers around them still and among us, and is to be seen amongst the reformers and philanthropists, who never contribute much to the improvement of society in any actual detail, but find a key principle for making the world anew and regenerating society. I have even seen faint signs of the same mysticism in social matters in some of the green-backers who have "thought out" in bed, as they relate, a scheme of wealth by paper money, as Mahomet would have received a surah or Joe Smith[1] a revelation about polygamy. Still there are limits to this resemblance, because in our nineteenth century American life a sense of humor, even if defective, answers some of the purposes of common sense.

Then again all the whimsical people who have hobbies of one sort or another come forward with projects which are the result of a strong impression, an individual misfortune, or an unregulated benevolent desire, and which are therefore the product of a facile emotion, not of a laborious investigation.

Then again the *dilettanti* make light work of social questions. Everyone, by the fact of living in society, gathers some observations of social phenomena. The belief grows up, as it was expressed some time ago by a professor of mathematics, that everybody knows about the topics of sociology. Those topics have a broad and generous character. They lend themselves easily to generalizations. There are as yet no sharp tests formulated. Above all, and worst lack of all as yet, we have no competent criticism. Hence it is easy for the aspirant after culture to venture on this field without great danger of being brought to account, as he would be if he attempted geology, or physics, or biology. Even a scientific man of high attainments in some other science, in which he well understands what special care, skill, and training are required, will not hesitate to dogmatize about a topic of sociology. A group of half-educated men may be relied upon to attack a social question and to hammer it dead in a few minutes with a couple of commonplaces and a sweeping *a*

[1] Joseph Smith (1805-1844) founded the religion of Mormonism which sanctioned polygamy. [S.P.]

priori assumption. Above all other topics, social topics lend themselves to the purposes of the diner-out.

Two facts, however, in regard to social phenomena need only be mentioned to be recognized as true. (1) Social phenomena always present themselves to us in very complex combinations, and (2) it is by no means easy to interpret the phenomena. The phenomena are often at three or four removes from their causes. Tradition, prejudice, fashion, habit, and other similar obstacles continually warp and deflect the social forces, and they constitute interferences whose magnitude is to be ascertained separately for each case. It is also impossible for us to set up a social experiment. To do that we should need to dispose of the time and liberty of a certain number of men. It follows that sociology requires a special method, and that probably no science requires such peculiar skill and sagacity in the observer and interpreter of the phenomena which are to be studied. One peculiarity may be especially noted because it shows a very common error of students of social science. A sociologist needs to arrange his facts before he has obtained them; that is to say, he must make a previous classification so as to take up the facts in a certain order. If he does not do this he may be overwhelmed in the mass of his material so that he never can master it. How shall anyone know how to classify until the science itself has made some progress? Statistics furnish us the best illustration at the present time of the difficulty here referred to.

When, now, we take into account these difficulties and requirements, it is evident that the task of sociology is one which will call for especial and long training, and that it will probably be a long time yet before we can train up any body of special students who will be so well trained in the theory and science of society as to be able to form valuable opinions on points of social disease and social remedy. But it is a fact of familiar observation that all popular discussions of social questions seize directly upon points of social disease and social remedies. The diagnosis of some asserted social ill and the prescription of the remedy are undertaken offhand by the first comer, and without reflecting that the diagnosis of a social disease is many times harder than that of a disease in an individual, and that to prescribe for a society is to prescribe for an organism which is immortal. To err in prescribing for a man is at worst to kill him; to err in prescribing for a society is to set in operation injurious forces which extend, ramify, and multiply their effects in ever new combinations throughout an indefinite future. It may pay to experiment with an individual, because he cannot wait for medical science to be perfected; it cannot pay to experiment with a society, because the society does not die and can afford to wait.

If we have to consider the need of sociology, innumerable reasons for studying it present themselves. In spite of all our acquisitions in natural science, the conception of a natural law—which is the most important good to be won from studying natural science—is yet exceedingly vague in the minds of ordinary intelligent people, and is very imperfect even amongst the educated. That conception is hardly yet applied by anybody to social facts and problems. Social questions force themselves upon us in multitudes every year as our civilization advances and our society becomes complex. When such questions arise they are wrangled over and tossed about without any orderly discussion, but as if they were only the sport of arbitrary whims. Is it not then necessary that we enable ourselves, by study of the facts and laws of society, to take up such questions from the correct point of view, and to proceed with the examination of them in such order and method that we can reach solid results, and thus obtain command of an increasing mass of knowledge about social phenomena? The assumption which underlies almost all discussion of social topics is that we men need only to make up our minds what kind of a society we want to have, and that then we can devise means for calling that society into existence. It is assumed that we can decide to live on one spot of the earth's surface or another, and to pursue there one industry or another, and then that we can, by our devices, make that industry as productive as any other could be in that place. People believe that we have only to choose whether we will have aristocratic institutions or democratic institutions. It is believed that statesmen can, if they will, put a people in the way of material prosperity. It is believed that rent on land can be abolished if it is not thought expedient to have it. It is assumed that peasant proprietors can be brought into existence anywhere where it is thought that it would be an advantage to have them. These illustrations might be multiplied indefinitely. They show the need of sociology, and if we should go on to notice the general conceptions of society, its ills and their remedies, which are held by various religious, political, and social sects, we should find ample further evidence of this need.

Let us then endeavor to define the field of sociology. Life in society is the life of a human society on this earth. Its elementary conditions are set by the nature of human beings and the nature of the earth. We have already become familiar, in biology, with the transcendent importance of the fact that life on earth must be maintained by a struggle against nature, and also by a competition with other forms of life. In the latter fact biology and sociology touch. Sociology is a science which deals with one range of phenomena produced by the struggle for existence, while biology deals with another. The forces are the same, acting on different fields and under different conditions. The sciences are truly cognate. Nature contains certain materials which are capable of satisfying human needs, but those materials must, with rare and mean exceptions, be won by labor, and must be fitted to human use by more labor. As soon as any number of human beings are struggling each to win from nature the material goods necessary to support life, and are carrying on this struggle side by side, certain social forces come into operation. The prime condition of this society will lie in the ratio of its numbers to the supply of materials within its reach. For the supply at any moment attainable is an exact quantity, and the number of persons who can be supplied is arithmetically limited. If the actual number present is very much less than the number who might be supported, the condition of all must be ample and easy. Freedom and facility mark all social relations under such a state of things. If the number is larger than that which can be supplied, the condition of all must be one of want and distress, or else a few must be well provided, the others being proportionately still worse off. Constraint, anxiety, possibly tyranny and repression, mark social relations. It is when the social pressure due to an unfavorable ratio of population to land becomes intense that the social forces develop increased activity. Division of labor, exchange, higher social organization, emigration, advance in the arts, spring from the necessity of contending against the harsher conditions of existence which are continually reproduced as the population surpasses the means of existence on any given status.

The society with which we have to deal does not consist of any number of men. An army is not a society. A man with his wife and his children constitutes a society, for its essential parts are all present, and the number more or less is immaterial. A certain division of labor between the sexes is imposed by nature. The family as a whole maintains itself better under an organization with division of labor than it could if the functions were shared so far as possible. From this germ the development of society goes on by the regular steps of advancement to higher organization, accompanied and sustained by improvements in the arts. The increase of population goes on according to biological laws which are capable of multiplying the species beyond any assignable limits, so that the number to be provided for steadily advances and the status of ease and abundance gives way to a status of want and constraint. Emigration is the first and simplest remedy. By winning more land the ratio of population to land is once more rendered favorable. It is to be noticed, however, that emigration is painful to all men. To the uncivilized man, to emigrate means to abandon a mass of experiences and traditions which have been won by suffering, and to go out to confront new hardships and perils. To the civilized man migration means cutting off old ties of kin and country. The earth has been peopled by man at the cost of this suffering.

On the side of the land also stands the law of the diminishing return as a limitation. More labor gets more from the land, but not proportionately more. Hence, if more men are to be supported, there is need not of a proportionate increase of labor, but of a disproportionate increase of labor. The law of population, therefore, combined with the law of the diminishing returns, constitutes the great underlying condition of society. Emigration, improvements in the arts, in morals, in education, in political organization are only stages in the struggle of man to meet these conditions, to break their force for a time, and to win room under them for ease and enlargement. Ease and enlargement mean either power to support more men on a given stage of comfort or power to advance the comfort of a given number of men. Progress is a word which has no meaning save in view of the laws of population and the diminishing return, and it is quite natural that anyone who fails to understand those laws should fall into doubt which way progress points, whether towards wealth or poverty. The laws of population and the diminishing return, in their combination, are the iron spur which has driven the race on to all which it has ever achieved, and the fact that population ever advances, yet advances against a barrier which resists more stubbornly at every step of advance, unless it is removed to a new distance by some conquest of man over nature, is the guarantee that the task of civilization will never be ended, but that the need for more energy, more intelligence, and more virtue will never cease while the race lasts. If it were possible for an increasing population to be sustained by proportionate increments of labor, we should all still be living in the original home of the race on the spontaneous products of the earth. Let him, therefore, who desires to study social phenomena first learn the transcendent importance for the whole social organization, industrial, political, and civil, of the ratio of population to land.

We have noticed that the relations involved in the struggle for existence are twofold. There is first the struggle of individuals to win the means of subsistence from nature, and secondly there is the competition of man with man in the effort to win a limited supply. The radical error of the socialists and sentimentalists is that they never distinguish these two relations from each other. They bring forward complaints which are really to be made, if at all, against the author of the universe for the hardships which man has to endure in his struggle with nature. The complaints are addressed, however, to society; that is, to other men under the same hardships. The only social element, however, is the competition of life, and when society is blamed for the ills which belong to the human lot, it is only burdening those who have successfully contended with those ills with the further task of conquering the same ills over again for somebody else. Hence liberty perishes in all socialistic schemes, and the tendency of such schemes is to the deterioration of society by burdening the good members and relieving the bad ones. The law of the survival of the fittest was not made by man and cannot be abrogated by man. We can only, by interfering with it, produce the survival of the unfittest. If a man comes forward with any grievance against the order of society so far as this is shaped by human agency, he must have patient hearing and full redress; but if he addresses a demand to society for relief from the hardships of life, he asks simply that somebody else should get his living for him. In that case he ought to be left to find out his error from hard experience.

The sentimental philosophy starts from the first principle that nothing is true which is disagreeable, and that we must not believe anything which is "shocking," no matter what the evidence may be. There are various stages of this philosophy. It touches on one side the intuitional philosophy which proves that certain things must exist by proving that man needs them, and it touches on the other side the vulgar socialism which affirms that the individual has a right to whatever he needs, and that this right is good against his fellow men. To this philosophy in all its grades the laws of population and the diminishing return have always been very distasteful. The laws which entail upon mankind an inheritance of labor cannot be acceptable to any philosophy which maintains that man comes into the world endowed with natural rights and is an inheritor of freedom. It is a death-blow to any intuitional philosophy to find out, as an historical fact, what diverse thoughts, beliefs, and actions man has manifested, and it requires but little actual knowledge of human history to show that the human race has never had any ease which it did not earn, or any freedom which it did not conquer. Sociology, therefore, by the investigations which it pursues, dispels illusions about what society is or may be, and gives instead knowledge of facts which are the basis of intelligent effort by man to make the best of his circumstances on earth. Sociology, therefore, which can never accomplish anything more than to enable us to make the best of our situation, will never be able to reconcile itself with those philosophies which are trying to find out how we may arrange things so as to satisfy any ideal of society.

The competition of life has taken the form, historically, of a struggle for the possession of the soil. In the simpler states of society the possession of the soil is tribal, and the struggles take place between groups, producing the wars and feuds which constitute almost the whole of early history. On the agricultural stage the tribal or communal possession of land exists as a survival, but it gives way to private property in land whenever the community advances and the institutions are free to mold themselves. The agricultural stage breaks up tribal relations and encourages individualization. This is one of the reasons why it is such an immeasurable advance over the lower forms of civilization. It sets free individual energy, and while the social bond gains in scope and variety, it also gains in elasticity, for the solidarity of the group is broken up and the individual may work out his own ends by his own means, subject only to the social ties which lie in the natural conditions of human life. It is only on the agricultural stage that liberty as civilized men understand it exists at all. The poets and sentimentalists, untaught to recognize the grand and world-wide cooperation which is secured by the free play of individual energy under the great laws of the social order, bewail the decay of early communal relations and exalt the liberty of the primitive stages of civilization. These notions all perish at the first touch of actual investigation. The whole retrospect of human history runs downwards towards beast-like misery and slavery to the destructive forces of nature. The whole history has been one series of toilsome, painful, and bloody struggles, first to find out where we were and what were the conditions of greater ease, and then to devise means to get relief. Most of the way the motives of advance have been experience of suffering and instinct. It is only in the most recent years that science has undertaken to teach without and in advance of suffering, and as yet science has to fight so hard against tradition that its authority is only slowly winning recognition. The institutions whose growth constitutes the advance of civilization have their guarantee in the very fact that they grew and became established. They suited man's purpose better than what went before. They are all imperfect, and all carry with them incidental ills, but each came to be because it was better than what went before, and each of which has perished, perished because a better one supplanted it.

It follows once and for all that to turn back to any defunct institution or organization because existing institutions are imperfect is to turn away from advance and is to retrograde. The path of improvement lies forwards. Private property in land, for instance, is an institution which has been developed in the most direct and legitimate manner. It may give way at a future time to some other institution which will grow up by imperceptible stages out of the efforts of men to contend successfully with existing evils, but the grounds for private property in land are easily perceived, and it is safe to say that no *a priori* scheme of state ownership or other tenure invented *en bloc* by any philosopher and adopted by legislative act will ever supplant it. To talk of any such thing is to manifest a total misconception of the facts and laws which it is the province of sociology to investigate. The case is less in magnitude but scarcely less out of joint with all correct principle when it is proposed to adopt a unique tax on land, in a country where the rent of land is so low that any important tax on land exceeds it, and therefore becomes indirect, and where also political power is in the hands of small landowners, who hold, without ever having formulated it, a doctrine of absolute property in the soil such as is not held by any other landowners in the world.

Sociology must exert a most important influence on political economy. Political economy is the science which investigates the laws of the material welfare of human societies. It is not its province to teach individuals how to get rich. It is a social science. It was the first branch of sociology which was pursued by man as a science. It is not strange that when the industrial organization of society was studied apart from the organism of which it forms a part it was largely dominated over by arbitrary dogmatism, and that it should have fallen into disrepute as a mere field of opinion, and of endless wrangling about opinions for which no guarantees could be given. The rise of a school of "historical" economists is itself a sign of a struggle towards a positive and scientific study of political economy, in its due relations to other social sciences, and this sign loses none of its significance in spite of the crudeness and extravagance of the opinions of the historical economists, and in spite of their very marked tendency to fall into dogmatism and hobby-riding. Political economy is thrown overboard by all groups and persons whenever it becomes troublesome. When it got in the way of Mr. Gladstone's land-bill he relegated it, by implication, to the planet Saturn, to the great delight of all the fair-traders, protectionists, soft-money men, and others who had found it in the way of their devices. What political economy needs in order to emerge from the tangle in which it is now involved, and to win a dignified and orderly development, is to find its field and its relations to other sciences fairly defined within the wider scope of sociology. Its laws will then take their place not as arbitrary or broken fragments, but in due relation to other laws. Those laws will win proof and establishment from this relation.

For instance, we have plenty of books, some of them by able writers, in which the old-fashioned Malthusian doctrine of population and the Ricardian law of rent are disputed because emigration, advance in the arts, etc., can offset the action of those laws or because those laws are not seen in action in the United States. Obviously no such objections ever could have been raised if the laws in question had been understood or had been put in their proper bearings. The Malthusian law of population and the Ricardian law of rent are cases in which by rare and most admirable acumen powerful thinkers perceived two great laws in particular phases of their action. With wider information it now appears that the law of population breaks the barriers of Malthus' narrower formulæ and appears as a great law of biology. The Ricardian law of rent is only a particular application of one of the great conditions of production. We have before us not special dogmas of political economy, but facts of the widest significance for the whole social development of the race. To object that these facts may be set aside by migration or advance in the arts is nothing to the purpose, for this is only altering the constants in the equation, which does not alter the form of the curve, but only its position relatively to some standard line. Furthermore, the laws themselves indicate that they have a maximum point for any society, or any given stage of the arts, and a condition of under-population, or of an extractive industry below its maximum, is just as consistent with the law as a condition of over-population and increasing distress. Hence inferences as to the law of population drawn from the status of an under-populated country are sure to be fallacious. In like manner arguments drawn from American phenomena in regard to rent and wages, when rent and wages are as yet only very imperfectly developed here, lead to erroneous conclusions. It only illustrates the unsatisfactory condition of political economy, and the want of strong criticism in it, that such arguments can find admission to its discussions and disturb its growth.

It is to the pursuit of sociology and the study of the industrial organization in combination with the other organizations of society that we must look for the more fruitful development of political economy. We are already in such a position with sociology that a person who has gained what we now possess of that science will bring to bear upon economic problems a sounder judgment and a more correct conception of all social relations than a person who may have read a library of the existing treatises on political economy. The essential elements of political economy are only corollaries or special cases of sociological principles. One who has command of the law of the conservation of energy as it manifests itself in society is armed at once against socialism, protectionism, paper money, and a score of other economic fallacies. The sociological view of political economy also includes whatever is sound in the dogmas of the "historical school" and furnishes what that school is apparently groping after.

As an illustration of the light which sociology throws on a great number of political and social phenomena which are constantly misconstrued, we may notice the differences in the industrial, political, and civil organizations which are produced all along at different stages of the ratio of population to land.

When a country is under-populated newcomers are not competitors, but assistants. If more come they may produce not only new quotas, but a surplus besides, to be divided between themselves and all who were present before. In such a state of things land is abundant and cheap. The possession of it confers no power or privilege. No one will work for another for wages when he can take up new land and be his own master. Hence it will pay no one to own more land than he can cultivate by his own labor, or with such aid as his own family supplies. Hence, again, land bears little or no rent; there will be no landlords living on rent and no laborers living on wages, but only a middle class of yeoman farmers. All are substantially on an equality, and democracy becomes the political form, because this is the only state of society in which the dogmatic assumption of equality, on which democracy is based, is realized as a fact. The same effects are powerfully reenforced by other facts. In a new and under-populated country the industries which are most profitable are the extractive industries. The characteristic of these, with the exception of some kinds of mining, is that they call for only a low organization of labor and small amount of capital. Hence they allow the workman to become speedily his own master, and they educate him to freedom, independence, and self-reliance. At the same time, the social groups being only vaguely marked off from each other, it is easy to pass from one class of occupations, and consequently from one social grade, to another. Finally, under the same circumstances education, skill, and superior training have but inferior value compared with what they have in densely populated countries. The advantages lie, in an under-populated country, with the coarser, unskilled, manual occupations, and not with the highest developments of science, literature, and art.

If now we turn for comparison to cases of over-population we see that the struggle for existence and the competition of life are intense where the pressure of population is great. This competition draws out the highest achievements. It makes the advantages of capital, education, talent, skill, and training tell to the utmost. It draws out the social scale upwards and downwards to great extremes and produces aristocratic social organizations

in spite of all dogmas of equality. Landlords, tenants (*i.e.,* capitalist employers), and laborers are the three primary divisions of
any aristocratic order, and they are sure to be developed whenever land bears rent and whenever tillage requires the application of large capital. At the same time liberty has to undergo
curtailment. A man who has a square mile to himself can easily
do as he likes, but a man who walks Broadway at noon or lives
in a tenement-house finds his power to do as he likes limited by
scores of considerations for the rights and feelings of his fellow
men. Furthermore, organization with subordination and discipline is essential in order that the society as a whole may win
a support from the land. In an over-populated country the extremes of wealth and luxury are presented side by side with the
extremes of poverty and distress. They are equally the products
of an intense social pressure. The achievements of power are
highest, the rewards of prudence, energy, enterprise, foresight,
sagacity, and all other industrial virtues is greatest; on the other
hand, the penalties of folly, weakness, error, and vice are most
terrible. Pauperism, prostitution, and crime are the attendants
of a state of society in which science, art, and literature reach
their highest developments. Now it is evident that over-population and under-population are only relative terms. Hence as
time goes on any under-populated nation is surely moving forward towards the other status, and is speedily losing its natural
advantages which are absolute, and also that relative advantage
which belongs to it if it is in neighborly relations with nations
of dense population and high civilization; *viz.,* the chance to
borrow and assimilate from them the products, in arts and
science, of high civilization without enduring the penalties
of intense social pressure.

We have seen that if we should try by any measures of arbitrary interference and assistance to relieve the victims of social
pressure from the calamity of their position we should only offer
premiums to folly and vice and extend them further. We have
also seen that we must go forward and meet our problems. We
cannot escape them by running away. If then it be asked what
the wit and effort of man can do to struggle with the problems
offered by social pressure, the answer is that he can do only

what his instinct has correctly and surely led him to do without
any artificial social organization of any kind, and that is, by improvements in the arts, in science, in morals, in political institutions, to widen and strengthen the power of man over nature.
The task of dealing with social ills is not a new task. People
set about it and discuss it as if the human race had hitherto
neglected it, and as if the solution of the problem was to be
something new in form and substance, different from the solution of all problems which have hitherto engaged human effort.
In truth, the human race has never done anything else but
struggle with the problem of social welfare. That struggle constitutes history, or the life of the human race on earth. That
struggle embraces all minor problems which occupy attention
here, save those of religion, which reaches beyond this world and
finds its objects beyond this life. Every successful effort to widen
the power of man over nature is a real victory over poverty,
vice, and misery, taking things in general and in the long run.
It would be hard to find a single instance of a direct assault
by positive effort upon poverty, vice, and misery which has not
either failed or, if it has not failed directly and entirely, has
not entailed other evils greater than the one which it removed.
The only two things which really tell on the welfare of man on
earth are hard work and self-denial (in technical language, labor
and capital), and these tell most when they are brought to bear
directly upon the effort to earn an honest living, to accumulate
capital, and to bring up a family of children to be industrious
and self-denying in their turn. I repeat that this is the way to
work for the welfare of man on earth; and what I mean to say
is that the common notion that when we are going to work for
the social welfare of man we must adopt a great dogma, organize for the realization of some great scheme, have before us an
abstract ideal, or otherwise do anything but live honest and industrious lives, is a great mistake. From the standpoint of the
sociologist pessimism and optimism are alike impertinent. To
be an optimist one must forget the frightful sanctions which are
attached to the laws of right living. To be a pessimist one must
overlook the education and growth which are the product of
effort and self-denial. In either case one is passing judgment on

what is inevitably fixed, and on which the approval or con-
demnation of man can produce no effect. The facts and laws
are, once and for all, so, and for us men that is the end of the
matter. The only persons for whom there would be any sense
in the question whether life is worth living are primarily the
yet unborn children, and secondarily the persons who are proposing to found families. For these latter the question would
take a somewat modified form: Will life be worth living for
children born of me? This question is, unfortunately, not put to
themselves by the appropriate persons as it would be if they had
been taught sociology. The sociologist is often asked if he wants
to kill off certain classes of troublesome and burdensome persons.
No such inference follows from any sound sociological doctrine,
but it is allowed to infer, as to a great many persons and classes,
that it would have been better for society, and would have involved no pain to them, if they had never been born.

In further illustration of the interpretation which sociology
offers of phenomena which are often obscure, we may note the
world-wide effects of the advances in the arts and sciences which
have been made during the last hundred years. These improvements have especially affected transportation and communication; that is, they have lessened the obstacles of time and space
which separate the groups of mankind from each other and have
tended to make the whole human race a single unit. The distinction between over-populated and under-populated countries loses
its sharpness, and all are brought to an average. Every person
who migrates from Europe to America affects the comparative
status of the two continents. He lessens the pressure in the
country he leaves and increases it in the country to which he
goes. If he goes to Minnesota and raises wheat there, which is
carried back to the country he left as cheap food for those who
have not emigrated, it is evident that the bearing upon social
pressure is twofold. It is evident, also, that the problem of social
pressure can no longer be correctly studied if the view is confined either to the country of immigration or the country of
emigration, but that it must embrace both. It is easy to see,
therefore, that the ratio of population to land with which we
have to deal is only in peculiar and limited cases that ratio as it

exists in England, Germany, or the United States. It is the ratio
as it exists in the civilized world, and every year that passes, as
our improved arts break down the barriers between different parts
of the earth, brings us nearer to the state of things where all the
population of Europe, America, Australasia, and South Africa
must be considered in relation to all the land of the same
territories, for all that territory will be available for all that
population, no matter what the proportion may be in which the
population is distributed over the various portions of the territory. The British Islands may become one great manufacturing
city. Minnesota, Texas, and Australia may not have five persons
to the square mile. Yet all will eat the meat of Texas and the
wheat of Minnesota and wear the wool of Australia manufac-
tured on the looms of England. That all will enjoy the maximum
of food and raiment under that state of things is as clear as
anything possibly can be which is not yet an accomplished fact.
We are working towards it by all our instincts of profit and improvement. The greatest obstacles are those which come from
prejudices, traditions, and dogmas, which are held independently
of any observation of facts or any correct reasoning, and which
set the right hand working against the left. For instance, the
Mississippi Valley was, a century ago, as unavailable to support
the population of France and Germany as if it had been in the
moon. The Mississippi Valley is now nearer to France and Germany than the British Islands were a century ago, reckoning
distance by the only true standard; viz., difficulty of communication. It is a fair way of stating it to say that the improvements
in transportation of the last fifty years have added to France and
Germany respectively a tract of land of the very highest fertility,
equal in area to the territory of those states, and available for
the support of their population. The public men of those countries are now declaring that this is a calamity, and are devising
means to counteract it.

The social and political effects of the improvements which
have been made must be very great. It follows from what we
have said about the effects of intense social pressure and high
competition that the effect of thus bringing to bear on the great
centers of population the new land of outlying countries must

be to relieve the pressure in the oldest countries and at the densest centers. Then the extremes of wealth and poverty, culture and brutality, will be contracted and there will follow a general tendency towards an average equality which, however, must be understood only within very broad limits. Such is no doubt the meaning of the general tendency towards equality, the decline of aristocratic institutions, the rise of the proletariat, and the ambitious expansion, in short, which is characteristic of modern civilized society. It would lead me too far to follow out this line of speculation as to the future, but two things ought to be noticed in passing. (1) There are important offsets to the brilliant promise which there is for mankind in a period during which, for the whole civilized world, there will be a wide margin of ease between the existing population and the supporting power of the available land. These offsets consist in (the effects of ignorance, error, and folly—the same forces which have always robbed mankind of half what they might have enjoyed on earth. Extravagant governments, abuses of public credit, wasteful taxation, legislative monopolies and special privileges, juggling with currency, restrictions on trade, wasteful armaments on land and sea, and other follies in economy and statecraft, are capable of wasting and nullifying all the gains of civilization. (2) The old classical civilization fell under an irruption of barbarians from without. It is possible that our new civilization may perish by an explosion from within.) The sentimentalists have been preaching for a century notions of rights and equality, of the dignity, wisdom, and power of the proletariat, which have filled the minds of ignorant men with impossible dreams. The thirst for luxurious enjoyment has taken possession of us all. It is the dark side of the power to foresee a possible future good with such distinctness as to make it a motive of energy and persevering industry—a power which is distinctly modern. Now the thirst for luxurious enjoyment, when brought into connection with the notions of rights, of power, and of equality, and dissociated from the notions of industry and economy, produces the notion that a man is robbed of his rights if he has not everything that he wants, and that he is deprived of equality if he sees anyone have more than he has, and that he is a fool if, having the power of the State in his

hands, he allows this state of things to last. Then we have socialism, communism, and nihilism; and the fairest conquests of
civilization, with all their promise of solid good to man, on the
sole conditions of virtue and wisdom, may be scattered to the
winds in a war of classes, or trampled underfoot by a mob which
can only hate what it cannot enjoy.

It must be confessed that sociology is yet in a tentative and
inchoate state. All that we can affirm with certainty is that social
phenomena are subject to law, and that the natural laws of the
social order are in their entire character like the laws of physics.
We can draw in grand outline the field of sociology and foresee
the shape that it will take and the relations it will bear to other
sciences. We can also already find the standpoint which it will
occupy, and, if a figure may be allowed, although we still look
over a wide landscape largely enveloped in mist, we can see
where the mist lies and define the general features of the landscape, subject to further corrections. To deride or contemn a
science in this state would certainly be a most unscientific proceeding. We confess, however, that so soon as we go beyond the
broadest principles of the science we have not yet succeeded in
discovering social laws, so as to be able to formulate them. A
great amount of labor yet remains to be done in the stages of
preparation. There are, however, not more than two or three
other sciences which are making as rapid progress as sociology,
and there is no other which is as full of promise for the welfare
of man. That sociology has an immense department of human
interests to control is beyond dispute. Hitherto this department
has been included in moral science, and it has not only been
confused and entangled by dogmas no two of which are consistent with each other, but also it has been without any growth,
so that at this moment our knowledge of social science is behind
the demands which existing social questions make upon us. We
are face to face with an issue no less grand than this: Shall we,
in our general social policy, pursue the effort to realize more
completely that constitutional liberty for which we have been
struggling throughout modern history, or shall we return to
the mediæval device of functionaries to regulate procedure and
to adjust interests? Shall we try to connect with liberty an equal

and appropriate responsibility as its essential complement and corrective, so that a man who gets his own way shall accept his own consequences, or shall we yield to the sentimentalism which, after preaching an unlimited liberty, robs those who have been wise out of pity for those who have been foolish? Shall we accept the inequalities which follow upon free competition as the definition of justice, or shall we suppress free competition in the interest of equality and to satisfy a baseless dogma of justice? Shall we try to solve the social entanglements which arise in a society where social ties are constantly becoming more numerous and more subtle, and where contract has only partly superseded custom and status, by returning to the latter, only hastening a more complete development of the former? These certainly are practical questions, and their scope is such that they embrace a great number of minor questions which are before us and which are coming up. It is to the science of society, which will derive true conceptions of society from the facts and laws of the social order,[2] studied without prejudice or bias of any sort, that we must look for the correct answer to these questions. By this observation the field of sociology and the work which it is to do for society are sufficiently defined.

[2] It has been objected that no proof is offered that social laws exist in the order of nature. By what demonstration could any such proof be given *a priori*? If a man of scientific training finds his attention arrested, in some group of phenomena, by these sequences, relations, and recurrences which he has learned to note as signs of action of law, he seeks to discover the law. If it exists, he finds it. What other proof of its existences could there be?

II

War

We have heard our political leaders say from time to time that "War is necessary," "War is a good thing." They were trying to establish a major premise which would suggest the conclusion, "Therefore let us have a little war now," or "It is wise, on general principles, to have a war once in a while." That argument may be taken as the text of the present essay. It has seemed to me worth while to show from the history of civilization just what war has done and has not done for the welfare of mankind.

In the eighteenth century it was assumed that the primitive state of mankind was one of Arcadian peace, joy, and contentment. In the nineteenth century the assumption went over to the other extreme—that the primitive state was one of universal warfare. This, like the former notion, is a great exaggeration. Man in the most primitive and uncivilized state known to us does not practice war all the time; he dreads it; he might rather be described as a peaceful animal. Real warfare comes with the collisions of more developed societies.

If we turn to facts about the least civilized men we find proofs that they are not warlike and do not practice war if they can help it. The Australians have no idea of conquest or battle. Their fights do not lead to slaughter or spoils or other consequences of victory.[1] Sometimes a fight takes the form of a friendly trial

[1] Curr, E. M.: The Australian Race, I, 86.

of skill with weapons between two parties who, one by one, cast their weapons at each other. Quarrels between tribes are sometimes settled by a single combat between chiefs. "Real fighting rarely takes place unless the women arouse the men," and even then it is only carried on by taunts and wrestling. "The first wound ends the combat." It is often followed by a war of words, hair-pulling, and blows with yam-sticks between the women.[2] The Australians have no war because they have no property that is worth pillaging; no tribe has anything to tempt the cupidity of another. They have no political organization, so there can be no war for power.[3] Each group appropriates hunting grounds, and over these war arises only with the increase of population. An Englishman who knew them well said that he knew of serious wounds, but he had known of but one death from their affrays.[4]

Neither are the Papuans of New Guinea warlike in all parts of the island. Like other men on the same grade of civilization, they may be assassins, but they are not warriors, and if two bodies of them meet in hostility, we are told that "there is a remarkably small death-roll at the end of the battle." [5] Of another group of them we are told that they have no offensive weapons at all, but live without disturbance from neighbors and without care for the future.[6] Their children rarely quarrel at play, and if they do, it ends in words. We are told that they lack the courage, temper, and concentration of will which would be necessary for a good schoolboy fight. Perhaps the converse would be true: they have no schoolboy fights and therefore have no courage, temper, and concentration of will. We are not astonished to hear that they develop excessive tyranny and cruelty to those who are weaker than themselves, especially to women, and even to their mothers.[7] These people are excessively distrustful of each other and villages but a little distance apart have very little intercourse. This is attributed in great part to head-hunting and cannibalism. In

[2] Dawson, J.: Australian Aborigines, 77.
[3] Semon, R.: In the Australian Bush, etc., 225.
[4] Smyth, R. B.: Aborigines of Victoria, I, 156, 160.
[5] Abel, C. W.: Savage Life in New Guinea, etc., 130.
[6] Krieger, M.: Neu-Guinea, 205.
[7] Pfeil, J.: Studien und Beobachtungen aus der Südsee, 23.

general they know the limits of their own territory and observe
them, but they quarrel about women.[8] The people in German
Melanesia are of the same kind; they are cowardly and mean,
make raids on each other's land to destroy and plunder, when
they think they can do it safely, but they will not join battle.[9]
On some of the small islands war is entirely unknown.[10]

The Chatham Islanders sometimes quarreled over booty won
in pursuing seals or whales, but they had a law that the first
drop of blood ended the fight.[11] The Khonds in Madras became
insubordinate a few years ago and a police force was sent against
them; they prepared stones to roll down the hill in front of their
village, but left the rear unguarded, and when the police entered
by the rear the Khonds protested against the unfairness of this
movement after they had taken such precautions in front.[12]
The Rengmahs on the Assam hills attach to the body a tail of
wood eighteen inches long, curved upwards, which they use to
wag defiance at an enemy.[13] Such people evidently could never
have had much experience of war. The Mrú on the Chittagong
hills are peaceable, timid, and simple; in a quarrel they do not
fight, but call in an exorcist to take the sense of the spirits on
the matter.[14]

Livingstone says that the tribes in the interior of South Africa,
where no slave trade existed, seldom had any war except about
cattle, and some tribes refused to keep cattle in order not to
offer temptation. In one case only had he heard of war for any
other reason; three brothers, Barolongs, fought over one woman,
and their tribe had remained divided, up to the time of writing,
into three parties. During his residence in the Bechuana country he never saw unarmed men strike each other. They quarrel
with words, but generally both parties burst into a laugh and

[8] Hagen, B.: Unter den Papua's, etc., 250.

[9] Pfeil, J.: l. c., 125.

[10] Kubary, J.: Beitrag zur Kenntnis der Núkuóro- oder Monteverde-Inseln,
20; Ibid.: Ethnographischer Beitrag zur Kenntnis des Karolinen Archipels, 94;
Bastian, A.: Die mikronesischen Kolonien, etc., 4.

[11] Weiss, B.: Mehr als fünfzig Jahre auf Chatham Island, 18.

[12] Journal of the Asiatic Society of Bombay ("J.A.S.B."), I, 240.

[13] Journal of the Anthropological Institute of Great Britain and Ireland
("J.A.I."), XI, 197.

[14] Lewin, T. H.: Wild Races of South-Eastern India, 232.

that ends it.[15] By an exception among the Canary islanders, the people of Hierro knew no war and had no weapons, although their long leaping-poles could be used as such when occasion demanded.[16]

A Spanish priest, writing an account, in 1739, of the Aurohuacos of Colombia,[17] says that they have no weapons of offense or defense. If two quarrel they go out to a big rock or tree and each with his staff beats the rock or tree with vituperations. The one whose staff breaks first is the victor; then they embrace and return home as friends. Even our American Indians, who appear in our legends to be so bloodthirsty and warlike, always appreciated the blessings of peace. Wampum strings and belts were associated with peace-pacts and with prayers for peace.

In contrast with these cases we find others of extreme warlikeness which account for the current idea that primitive men love war and practice it all the time. But if we examine the cases of peacefulness or unwarlikeness which have been cited, we see that only two or three seem to present evidence of Arcadian peace and simplicity, such as, in the imagination of the eighteenth century philosophers, characterized men in a state of nature. Probably if we had fuller knowledge these few instances would be much modified. What we see is that men have always quarreled. The cases which have been selected are some of them also those of people who have been defeated, broken, and cowed down. Another set of examples consists of those in which abstinence from war is due to cowardice, and with it go the vices of cowardice—tyranny and cruelty to the weak. These cases are calculated to delight the hearts of the advocates of strenuosity. What our testimonies have in common is this: they show that we cannot postulate a warlike character or a habit of fighting as a universal or even characteristic trait of primitive man.

When we undertake to talk about primitive society we should conceive of it as consisting of petty groups scattered separately over a great territory. I speak of groups because I want a term

[15] Livingstone, D.: Missionary Travels and Researches in South Africa, I, 232; II, 503.

[16] American Anthropologist, N. S., II, 475.

[17] Ibid., N. S. III, 612.

of the widest significance. The group may consist, as it does amongst Australians and Bushmen, of a man with one or possibly two wives and their children, or it may have a few more members, or it may be a village group as in New Guinea, or a tribe or part of a tribe as amongst our own Indians. It is to be observed that this ultimate unit is a group and not an individual. Every individual excludes every other in the competition of life unless they can by combining together win more out of nature by joint effort than the sum of what they could win separately. This combination is what makes groups and brings about industrial organization. When a man and woman unite in the most elementary group known, they do it for economic reasons, because they can carry on the struggle for existence better together than apart. In time this turns into a kin-group, united "by blood." This remains undivided as long as its organization gives advantages, but breaks up when it grows too big for the existing economic system. As soon as it breaks, the fractions begin to compete with each other. If by greater culture a higher organization becomes possible, two groups coalesce by intermarriage or conquest, competition gives way to combination again, and the bigger unit enters into competition with other composite units. Thus at all stages throughout the history of civilization competition and combination forever alternate with each other.

These groups are independent of each other, their size being determined by their mode of life, because the number who can live together economically is limited by the possibilities of the food-quest. When a group outgrows this limit, it breaks up and scatters. The fact of former association is long remembered and there is a bond of kinship and alliance which may at times draw former associates together again for festivals and religious observances, but after they separate the tendency is to become entirely independent and to fall under the type just described; viz., scattered groups each with its individuality, yet in a certain neighborhood to each other. Their remoter relationship does not keep them from quarreling and fighting. In the book of Judges[18] we see cases of war between tribes of Israel in spite of the higher

[18] Chapters 12, 20.

bond which united them with each other and separated them from the Gentiles.

All the members of one group are comrades to each other, and have a common interest against every other group. If we assume a standpoint in one group we may call that one the "we-group" or the "in-group"; then every other group is to us an "others-group" or an "out-group." The sentiment which prevails inside the "we-group," between its members, is that of peace and co-operation; the sentiment which prevails inside of a group towards all outsiders is that of hostility and war. These two sentiments are perfectly consistent with each other; in fact, they necessarily complement each other. Let us see why that is so.

War arises from the competition of life, not from the struggle for existence. In the struggle for existence a man is wrestling with nature to extort from her the means of subsistence. It is when two men are striving side by side in the struggle for existence, to extort from nature the supplies they need, that they come into rivalry and a collision of interest with each other takes place. This collision may be light and unimportant, if the supplies are large and the number of men small, or it may be harsh and violent, if there are many men striving for a small supply. This collision we call the competition of life. Of course men are in the competition of life with beasts, reptiles, insects, and plants—in short, with all organic forms; we will, however, confine our attention to men. The greater or less intensity of the competition of life is a fundamental condition of human existence, and the competition arises between those ultimate unit groups which I have described. The members of the unit group work together. The Australian or Bushman hunter goes abroad to seek meat food, while the woman stays by the fire at a trysting place, with the children, and collects plant food. They cooperate in the struggle for existence, and the size of the group is fixed by the number who can work together to the greatest advantage under their mode of life. Such a group, therefore, has a common interest. It must have control of a certain area of land; hence it comes into collision of interest with every other group. The competition of life, therefore, arises between groups, not be-

tween individuals, and we see that the members of the in-group
are allies and joint-partners in one interest while they are brought
into antagonism of interest with all outsiders. It is the competition of life, therefore, which makes war, and that is why war
always has existed and always will. It is in the conditions of
human existence. In the cases which have been cited of nature
peoples who have no war, we have heard mention already of
division of hunting grounds and of quarrels which arise about
them. Wherever there is no war, there we find that there is no
crowding, as among the scattered Eskimo, or that, after long
fighting, treaties and agreements have been made to cover all
relations of interest between the groups. These we call peace-
pacts, and it is evident that they consist in conventional agreements creating some combination between the groups which are
parties to the agreement.

Each group must regard every other as a possible enemy on
account of the antagonism of interests, and so it views every
other group with suspicion and distrust, although actual hostilities occur only on specific occasion. Every member of another
group is a stranger; he may be admitted as a guest, in which case
rights and security are granted him, but if not so admitted he is
an enemy. We can now see why the sentiments of peace and
cooperation inside are complementary to sentiments of hostility
outside. It is because any group, in order to be strong against
an outside enemy, must be well disciplined, harmonious, and
peaceful inside; in other words, because discord inside would
cause defeat in battle with another group. Therefore the same
conditions which made men warlike against outsiders made them
yield to the control of chiefs, submit to discipline, obey law, cultivate peace, and create institutions inside. The notion of rights
grows up in the in-group from the usages established there
securing peace. There was a double education, at the same time,
out of the same facts and relations. It is no paradox at all to say
that peace makes war and that war makes peace. There are two
codes of morals and two sets of mores, one for comrades inside
and the other for strangers outside, and they arise from the
same interests. Against outsiders it was meritorious to kill, plunder, practice blood revenge, and to steal women and slaves; but

inside none of these things could be allowed because they would produce discord and weakness. Hence, in the in-group, law (under the forms of custom and taboo) and institutions had to take the place of force. Every group was a peace-group inside and the peace was sanctioned by the ghosts of the ancestors who had handed down the customs and taboos. Against outsiders religion sanctioned and encouraged war; for the ghosts of the ancestors, or the gods, would rejoice to see their posterity and worshipers once more defeat, slay, plunder, and enslave the ancient enemy.

The Eskimos of Bering Strait think it wrong to steal from people in the same village or tribe; a thief is publicly reproached and forced to return the thing stolen. But to steal from an outsider is not wrong unless it brings harm on one's own tribe.[19] Strabo[20] says of the Scythians that they were just and kind to each other, but very savage towards all outsiders. The sentiment of cohesion, internal comradeship, and devotion to the in-group, which carries with it a sense of superiority to any out-group and readiness to defend the interests of the in-group against the out-group, is technically known as ethnocentrism. It is really the sentiment of patriotism in all its philosophic fullness; that is, both in its rationality and in its extravagant exaggeration. The Mohaves and the Seri of southern California will have no relations of marriage or trade with any other people; they think themselves superior. The Mohaves are wild and barbarous and the Seri are on a lower grade of civilization than any other tribe in America. Therefore, we see that ethnocentrism has nothing to do with the relative grade of civilization of any people. The Seri think that "the brightest virtue is the shedding of alien blood, while the blackest crime in their calendar is alien conjugal union." [21] Perhaps nine-tenths of all the names given by savage tribes to themselves mean "Men," "The Only Men," or "Men of Men"; that is, We are men, the rest are something else. A recent etymology of the word Iroquois makes it mean "I am the real man." [22] In general Indians held that they were a favored

[19] Bureau of American Ethnology, 18, I, 293.
[20] 300, 302.
[21] Bur. Eth., 17, I, 11; Am. Anth., N. S., IV, 279.
[22] Am. Anth., N. S., IV, 558.

race, due to a special creation.[23] Nansen[24] gives a letter written
by an Eskimo in 1756 when he heard of the war between England
and France. He burst into a rhapsody about Greenland. "Your
unfruitfulness makes us happy and saves us from molestation."
The writer was surprised that the Christians had not learned
better manners amongst the Eskimo, and he proposed to send
missionaries to them. A traveler in Formosa says that the For-
mosans thought foreigners barbarians, "civilization being solely
within the dominion of the Celestial Emperor. All the rest of
the world—if there was any poor remainder—was benighted,
and but the home of 'barbarians,' not 'men.'"[25] This is the
language of ethnocentrism; it may be read in the newspapers
of any civilized country to-day.

We find then that there are two sentiments in the minds of
the same men at the same time. These have been called militancy
and industrialism. The latter term does not seem to be a good
one and it is not apt until we reach high civilization; what we
want is a term to express the peace sentiment in antithesis to
militancy, but industrialism has obtained currency and it has
this much justification, even for savage life, that, inside the
group, the needs of life must be provided for by productive labor.
Generally that is left to the women and the men practice milita-
rism.

It would not be possible for neighboring groups to remain
really isolated from each other. One has in its territory stone
or salt, water or fuel, limited fruits, melons, nuts, fish, or perhaps
other natural materials which the others need. They also take
wives from each other, generally, but not always. Hence arise
treaties of *commercium* and *connubium,* which bring about a
middle state of things between war and peace. These treaties are
the origin of international law. A comparison of modern municipal and international law will show that the difference between
the relations of members of the in-group with each other, and
of the groups with each other, still exists.

If now we turn back to the question with which I started,

[23] Bur. Eth., VIII, 36.
[24] Eskimo Life, 180.
[25] Pickering, W. A.: **Pioneering in Formosa**, 136.

whether men began in a state of peace or a state of war, we see the answer. They began with both together. Which preponderated is a question of the intensity of the competition of life at the time. When that competition was intense, war was frequent and fierce, the weaker were exterminated or absorbed by the stronger, the internal discipline of the conquerors became stronger, chiefs got more absolute power, laws became more stringent, religious observances won greater authority, and so the whole societal system was more firmly integrated. On the other hand, when there were no close or powerful neighbors, there was little or no war, the internal organization remained lax and feeble, chiefs had little power, and a societal system scarcely existed.

The four great motives which move men to social activity are hunger, love, vanity, and fear of superior powers. If we search out the causes which have moved men to war we find them under each of these motives or interests. Men have fought for hunting grounds, for supplies which are locally limited and may be monopolized, for commerce, for slaves, and probably also for human flesh. These motives come under hunger, or the food-quest, or more widely under the economic effort to win subsistence. They have fought for and on account of women, which we must put partly under love, although the women were wanted chiefly as laborers and so, along with the slaves, would come under the former head. They have fought to win heads, or scalps, or other trophies, and for honor or dignity, or purely for glory; this comes under the operation of vanity. They have fought for blood revenge, to prevent or punish sorcery, and to please their gods; these motives belong under the fear of superior powers. It was reserved for modern civilized men to fight on account of differences of religion, and from this motive the fiercest and most persistent wars have been waged.

Is there anything grand or noble in any of these motives of war? Not a bit. But we must remember that the motives from which men act have nothing at all to do with the consequences of their action. Where will you find in history a case of a great purpose rationally adopted by a great society and carried through to the intended result and then followed by the expected consequences in the way of social advantage? You can find no such thing. Men act from immediate and interested motives like these for which they have waged war, and the consequences come out of the forces which are set loose. The consequences may be advantageous or disadvantageous to men. The story of these acts and consequences makes up human history. So it has been with war. While men were fighting for glory and greed, for revenge and superstition, they were building human society. They were acquiring discipline and cohesion; they were learning cooperation, perseverance, fortitude, and patience. Those are not savage virtues; they are products of education. War forms larger social units and produces states; of the North American Indians, those had the intensest feeling of unity who were the most warlike.[26] The Netherlands form a striking example in modern history of the weakness of a state which is internally divided; the best historian of Dutch civilization tells us that the internal disintegration was always greatest in times of truce or of peace.[27] There can be no doubt that the Germans of to-day owe their preeminence in industry and science to the fact that they are a highly disciplined nation. A Portuguese sociologist says that "War is the living fountain from which flows the entire society." [28] If we fix our minds on the organic growth and organization of society, this assertion is not exaggerated. An American sociologist[29] says that "in spite of the countless miseries which follow in its train, war has probably been the highest stimulus to racial progress. It is the most potent excitant known to all the faculties." The great conquests have destroyed what was effete and opened the way for what was viable. What appalls us, however, is the frightful waste of this process of evolution by war—waste of life and waste of capital. It is this waste which has made the evolution of civilization so slow.)

Here, then, let us turn back and see how the peace-element develops alongside the war-element. We shall find that peace-rules and peace-institutions have been established, from the

---

[26] Am. Anth., N. S., IV, 279.
[27] Van Duyl, C. F.: Overzicht der Beschavingsgeschiedenis van het Nederlandsche Volk, 190.
[28] Martins, J. P. Oliveira: As Raças Humanas, etc., II, 55.
[29] Brinton, D. G.: Races and Peoples, 76.

earliest civilization, even for the relations of groups with each other. House-peace is perhaps the simplest form. The nature-people very often bury a man under his own fireplace, and from this usage radiate various customs, all of which go to associate the ghosts of the dead with the hearthstone of the living. It follows that quarreling, brawling, or violence near the hearth is an insult to the ghosts. Hence arises a notion of religious sacredness about the hearth, an atmosphere of peace is created, and the women who live in the house and work at the hearth profit by it. The householder has a dignity and prerogative in his house, however humble his social position may be, hence the maxim that a man's house is his castle goes back to the beginning of civilization. It may be only a wind-shelter, but the ghosts protect it; and any stranger, fugitive, suppliant, even an enemy, if admitted, comes under the house protection and hospitality while there. As the house becomes larger and better the peace-taboo extends from the fireplace to the whole house and then to the yard or enclosure. This is the house-peace.

If any group which possesses deposits of salt, flint-stone fit for implements, pipe-stone, water supply, or special foods should try to prevent others from having access to the same, all others would join in war against that one until an agreement was made and established by usage. This agreement is either one of peaceful access to natural supplies or one of trade. Tribes also agree to take wives from each other. We often have reason to be astonished at the institution-making power of nature-men when disagreeable experience has forced them to find relief. The Tubu of the Sahara are warlike and distrustful even of each other to such an extent that they scarcely form a society; even in their villages they quarrel and fight. It is a very noteworthy feature that these people have no notion of rights. It is the in-group as a peace-group which is the school of rights; as we have seen, there can be peace and order inside only by law (using this term in its broadest sense); but a law creates and enforces rights. Now these Tubu have been forced to make a law that inside the village no weapons may be worn,[30] so that here already we find an institutional arrangement to limit warlikeness. When Nachti-

[30] Nachtigal, G.: Sahara und Sudan, I, 439.

gal, visiting the Tubu, complained of their ill usage of himself
and threatened to go away, they pointed out to him that as soon
as he had left their territory he would be at their mercy.[31] This
shows that even they had an idea of some rights of a guest inside
their group as compared with his status outside, when he would
be protected by nothing. The Beduin have the same notion.
They are ruthless robbers and murderers, but a guest in the tent
is perfectly safe and entitled to their best hospitality. When he
leaves it he is fair game, whether enemy, friend, or neighbor.[32]

The West-Australians have a usage that any man who has committed a wrong according to their code must submit to a flight
of spears from all who think themselves aggrieved, or he must
allow a spear to be thrust through his leg or arm. There is a
tariff of wounds as penalties for all common crimes.[33] We understand that this is an in-group usage. It is a common custom in
Australia that a man who has stolen a wife from an out-group
must submit to a flight of spears from her group-comrades; this
is now only a ceremony, but it is a peace-institution which has
set aside old warfare on account of stolen women. As we have
seen, the Australians live in very small groups, but they assemble
from time to time in large kin-groups for purposes of festivals of
a religious character. The kin-groups are not peace-groups,[34] because they are loose and have no common life. At the assemblies
all the sacred objects are brought into the ceremonial ground,
but on account of the danger of quarrels, no display of arms is
allowed anywhere near the sacred objects.[35] Bearers of messages
from one tribe to another are regarded as under a peace-taboo in
eastern Australia; women are under a peace-taboo and hence
are employed as ambassadors to arrange disputes between tribes.
After a quarrel there is a corroboree, to make and confirm
peace.[36] These usages are institutional. They are positive rules

[31] *Ibid.*, I, 276.
[32] Burchardt, J. L.: Notes on the Bedouins, etc., 90.
[33] Grey, G.: Journals of Two Expeditions of Discovery in North-West and
Western Australia, II, 243.
[34] Curr: Australian Race, I, 69.
[35] Spencer, B., and Gillen, F. J.: Native Tribes of Central Australia, 135.
[36] Mathews, R. H.: Message-sticks used by the Aborigines of Australia, in
Am. Anth., X, 290; Smyth, R. B.: Aborigines of Victoria, I, 165, 181; Curr,
Australian Race, I, 92.

of an arbitrary character, depending upon agreement and usage, but are devised to satisfy expediency. In Queensland no fighting at all is allowed at night in camp; those who want to fight must go outside, and after a fight the victor must show to his comrades that he had a real grievance. If he does not convince them of this they force him to submit to the same mutilation from his victim that he has inflicted. The women fight with their yam-sticks, which are about four feet long. One woman allows the other to strike her on the head; the second must then submit to a blow; thus they go on until one does not want any more.[37] What we have to notice here is that the fight, inside the group, is under regulations, which fact makes it institutional. The duel is a similar case of a conventionalized fight in the midst of a peaceful civil order. In all these cases we see that war is admitted inside of a peace-group when individuals are wronged or offended by comrades, but only in conventionalized and regulated form, so that it is a kind of lawful war.

We also find war between groups under some regulation and conventionalization when there is a bond of kinship or religion uniting the two groups. It appears that this is the origin of the rules of war by which its horrors are reduced. On the island of Tanna in the New Hebrides the eight thousand inhabitants are divided into two groups, one at each end of the island, and each group is subdivided into villages. If two villages in the same division fight, as they often do, the fighting is not intense and there is no cannibalism; but between the two big divisions there is blood revenge, and if they fight there is no limit to the ferocity, cannibalism being then practiced.[38] On the Mortlock Islands when two tribes go to war each warrior must select as his antagonist on the other side one who is not in the same kin-group with himself.[39] Amongst certain Sumatrans if a man of one village has a grievance against a man of another, the men of the former go into the fields of the other, where they are met by the local chief, who asks their errand. They answer that they have

[37] Roth, W. E.: Ethnological Studies among the North-West-Central Queensland Aborigines, 141.

[38] Australian Association for the Advancement of Science, 1892, 648.

[39] Finsch, O.: Ethnologische Erfahrungen und Belegstücke aus der Südsee, III, 311.

come to destroy the plantation of the man in the village who has injured a man of theirs. The chief admits that this is just, but proposes to avoid violence; so he brings to them fruit from the plantation of the offender and, if the offense was great, he allows them to destroy a certain number of trees on it. They also burn down the offender's house "ceremonially"—a little hut is built of light material on his field and with triumphant cries is set on fire by the offended party. Generally an agreement is reached, but if not, long hostilities endure between two neighboring villages.[40]

The Christian states have always professed to moderate somewhat the horrors of war when they went to fighting with each other, and so we have laws of war which are good between the states agreeing to them, but not with outsiders. This makes a limited peace-group of all the states which unite now to make international law. Let us follow these peace-institutions up into higher civilization.

The Scandinavian people spread in small bodies over their territory, and these bodies often engaged in war with each other. They had a common sanctuary at Upsala at which there were annual festivals. This religious bond kept up a certain sense of national unity, which, however, has never produced national sympathy. At the festivals at Upsala peace was enforced for the time and place[41]; disputes were settled and fairs held, and there were also feasts and conferences. The Swedes in the thirteenth century formed kin-groups which adopted rules of mutual succor and defense.[42] The dwellings of kings also came to have in so far the character of sanctuaries that peace was maintained around them.[43] The ancient Germans maintained by law and severe penalties peace for women as to person and property; the penalties for wrong to a woman varied in the laws of the different German nations, but were two or three times as great as for wrongs to men.[44] The house-peace was also very fully

---

[40] Snouck-Hurgronje, C. S.: De Atjèhers, I, 81-83.
[41] Geijer, E. G.: Svenska Folkets Historia, I, 12, 112.
[42] Montelius, O.: Sveriges Historia, I, 461.
[43] Folklore, 1900, 285.
[44] Stammler, C.: Ueber die Stellung der Frauen im alten deutschen Recht,

9.

developed in German law.[45] The Peace of God was perhaps
the most remarkable case in history of a law to establish a time-
taboo against war and violence. In the tenth century the church
tried to curb the robber barons and to protect merchants; the
attempts were often repeated with little result, but the "Truce of
God" was at last established in 1041 by the Bishop of Arles and
the Abbot of Cluny, and it won some acceptance throughout
France. There was to be no fighting between Wednesday evening
and Monday morning; later these limits were changed.[46] No such
law was ever obeyed with any precision and it never became a
custom, much less an institution, but it had some influence. As
the kings gained real power and prestige in the feudal states they
made the king's peace a great reality; it went with the development of the modern state. The king's peace was a name for a
central civil authority which could put down all private war
and violations of public order and establish a peace-group over
a great extent of territory, within which rights, law, and civil
authority should be secured by competent tribunals. In the
Holy Roman Empire of the German nation the public general
peace of the empire was introduced in 1495, but the emperors
never had the means to enforce it, and it did not exist until 1873.
We can see how the king's peace grew by the following case:
Canute the Dane made a law in England that, if any unknown
man was found dead, he should be assumed to be a Dane and a
special tax, called *murdrum,* should be paid for him to the king.
William the Conqueror followed this example, only the unknown man was assumed to be a Norman; if it could be proved
that he was an Englishman ("proving his Englishry") then the
murderer or the hundred had nothing to pay to the king but
only the legal compensation to the family of the deceased, if he
had one.[47] This means that the king first extended his peace
over his own countrymen by a special penalty on the murder of
one of them, while Englishmen were left only under the old law
of composition for blood revenge; but in time equal protection
was extended to all his subjects. Again, at the time of the Con-

[45] Osenbrüggen, E.: Der Hausfrieden.
[46] Van Duyl, C. F.: Beschavingsgeschiedenis, etc., 110.
[47] Inderwick, F. A.: The King's Peace, 27.

quest all crimes committed on the roads which ran through a city (Canterbury, for instance) were crimes against the king's peace—which also extended one league, three perches, and three feet beyond the city gate. This means that the high roads which ran through a town were first brought under the king's peace, and this peace also extended beyond the royal burgh for an extent which was measured with droll accuracy. What was a crime elsewhere was a greater crime there, and what was not a crime elsewhere might be a crime there. King Edmund forbade blood revenge in his burgh;[48] that is, he delimited an in-group in which there must be law and an administration of justice by his tribunal; Jews and merchants bought the protection of the king's peace throughout his realm. From this germ grew up the state as a peace-group and the king's peace as the law of the land; we Americans call it the peace of the people.

One of the most remarkable examples of a peace-group which could be mentioned is the League of the Iroquois which was formed in the sixteenth century; it deserves to be classed here with the peace-institutions of civilized states. This league was a confederation of five, afterwards six tribes of Indians, to maintain peace. By Indian usage blood revenge was a duty; but the Iroquois confederation put a stop to this, as between its members, by substituting laws and civil authority. It was, for its stage, fully as marvelous a production of statesmanship as are these United States—themselves a great peace-confederation. Compared with Algonkins and Sioux the Iroquois were an industrial society. They tried to force others to join the confederacy—that is, to come into the peace-pact or to make an alliance with it; if they would do neither, war arose and the outside people was either exterminated or absorbed.[49] Hiawatha was the culture-hero to whom the formation of the league was attributed. The constitution was held in memory by strings of wampum, and at annual festivals there were confessions and exhortations. The duties inculcated were those of a warrior towards outsiders and of tribal

[48] Maitland, F. W.: Domesday Book and Beyond, 184.
[49] Hale, H.: The Iroquois Book of Rites (in Brinton, D. G.: Library of Aboriginal American Literature, No. II), 68, 70, 92; Morgan, L. H.: League of the Iroquois, 91.

brotherhood towards insiders. "The duty of living in harmony
and peace, of avoiding evil-speaking, of kindness to the orphan,
of charity to the needy and of hospitality to all, would be among
the prominent topics brought under consideration" at the annual
assemblies.[50]

We have now found a peace of the house, of the sanctuary, of
religion, of the market, of women, of the popular assembly, and
of the king, all of which were legal and institutional checks upon
war and an introduction of rational and moral methods in the
place of force. Let us see next what has been the relation between religion on the one side and peace or war on the other.

Those who perform the rites of worship towards the same ancestors or the same gods come into the same cult-group, but no
religion has ever succeeded in making its cult-group into a
peace-group, although they all try to do it. The salutation of
members of a cult-group to each other is very generally "Peace,"
or something equivalent. Quakers call themselves "Friends" and
always have a closer bond to each other than to the outside
world. Such a peace-group is only an ideal for all who profess
the same religion; in most of the great religions down to the
seventeenth century, dissenters or heretics were always treated
with great severity, because it was thought that they would bring
down the wrath of the ghost or the god not only on themselves
but also on the whole community. The New England Puritans
had this notion that the sins of some would bring down the
wrath of God on the whole. Religion has always intensified
ethnocentrism; the adherents of a religion always think themselves the chosen people or else they think that their god is
superior to all others, which amounts to the same thing. The
Jews looked down upon all non-Jews as Gentiles; the Mohammedans despise all infidels—their attitude towards non-Mussul-
mans is one leading to aggression, plunder, and annihilation.
The Greeks looked down on all non-Greeks as barbarians, but
in their case the sentiment was only partly religious; they themselves were never united by their own religion. In the thirteenth
and fourteenth centuries, when Mohammedanism threatened to

[50] Morgan, L. H.: League of the Iroquois, 190; Hale, H.: Iroquois Book of
Rites, 32.

overwhelm Christendom, Latin Christians were inflamed with greater rage against Greek Christians than against Mohammedans. Nicholas V in 1452 gave to Alfonso V of Portugal authority to subjugate any non-Christians, having in view especially people of the west coast of Africa, and to reduce them to servitude (*illorum personas in servitutem*), which probably did not mean slavery, but subjection.[51] The Spaniards and Portuguese of the sixteenth century treated all aborigines with ruthlessness because the aborigines were outside of Christianity and entitled to no rights or consideration. When the American colonies revolted, the English were amazed that the colonists could ally themselves with Frenchmen against the mother-country, although the French were Roman Catholics in religion, absolutists in the state, and of an alien nationality. Buddhism is characterized by a pervading peacefulness, but no religion has ever kept its adherents from fighting each other. The instances which have been cited suffice to show that religion has been quite as much a stimulus to war as to peace; and religious wars are proverbial for ruthlessness and ferocity.

Christianity has always contained an ideal of itself as a peace-group. The mediæval church tried to unite all Christendom into a cult- and peace-group which should reach over all the disintegration and war of the feudal period. This was the sense of mediæval Catholicity. Churches, convents, and ecclesiastical persons were put under a peace-taboo. The church, however, at the same time, entered into an alliance with the feudal nobles and adopted militant methods; heretics were dealt with as outside the fold. The modern state, as it began to take definite form, entered into a contest with the church for the control of society and for the guardianship of peace, because the church had failed to secure peace.

The United States presents us a case quite by itself. We have here a confederated state which is a grand peace-group. It occupies the heart of a continent; therefore there can be no question of balance of power here and no need of war preparations such as now impoverish Europe. The United States is a new country with a sparse population and no strong neighbors. Such

---

[51] Raynaldus, O.: Annales Ecclesiasticae, etc., 18, 423.

a state will be a democracy and a republic, and it will be "free" in almost any sense that its people choose. If this state becomes militant, it will be because its people choose to become such; it will be because they think that war and warlikeness are desirable in themselves and are worth going after. On their own continent they need never encounter war on their path of industrial and political development up to any standard which they choose to adopt. It is a very remarkable fact, and one which has had immense influence on the history of civilization, that the land of the globe is divided into two great sections, the mass of Europe, Asia, and Africa on the one side and these two Americas on the other, and that one of these worlds remained unknown to the other until only four hundred years ago. We talk a great deal about progress and modern enlightenment and democracy and the happiness of the masses, but very few people seem to know to what a great extent all those things are consequences of the discovery of the new world. As to this matter of war which we are now considering, the fact that the new world is removed to such a distance from the old world made it possible for men to make a new start here. It was possible to break old traditions, to revise institutions, and to think out a new philosophy to fit an infant society, at the same time that whatever there was in the inheritance from the old world which seemed good and available might be kept. It was a marvelous opportunity; to the student of history and human institutions it seems incredible that it ever could have been offered. The men who founded this republic recognized that opportunity and tried to use it. It is we who are now here who have thrown it away; we have decided that instead of working out the advantages of it by peace, simplicity, domestic happiness, industry and thrift, we would rather do it in the old way by war and glory, alternate victory and calamity, adventurous enterprises, grand finance, powerful government, and great social contrasts of splendor and misery. Future ages will look back to us with amazement and reproach that we should have made such a choice in the face of such an opportunity and should have entailed on them the consequences—for the opportunity will never come again.

Some illustration of our subject has, however, been furnished by the internal history of our peace-group. The aborigines of this continent have never been taken into our peace-bond, and our law about them is, consequently, full of inconsistencies. Sometimes they have been treated as comrades in the in-group; sometimes as an out-group with which our group was on a footing of hostility. Another question seems to be arising with respect to the Negroes; we have been trying, since the Civil War, to absorb them into our peace-bond, but we have not succeeded. They are in it and not of it now, as much as, or more than, in the days of slavery, for the two races live more independently of each other now than they did in those former days. The Southern States do not constitute true societies because they lack unity of interest and sentiment, on account of the race difference which divides them. This discord may prove worse and more fatal to the internal integrity of the peace-group than such old antagonisms of interest as disturb Ireland, the national antagonisms which agitate Austria-Hungary, or the religious antagonisms which distract Belgium. In short, a state needs to be a true peace-group in which there is sufficient concord and sympathy to overcome the antagonisms of nationality, race, class, etc., and in which are maintained institutions adequate to adjust interests and control passions. Before even the great civilized states have reached this model, there is yet much to be done.

If we look at these facts about peace-laws and institutions and the formation of peace-groups in connection with the facts previously presented about the causes of war and the taste for war, we see that militancy and peacefulness have existed side by side in human society from the beginning just as they exist now. A peaceful society must be industrial because it must produce instead of plundering; it is for this reason that the industrial type of society is the opposite of the militant type. In any state on the continent of Europe to-day these two types of societal organization may be seen interwoven with each other and fighting each other. Industrialism builds up; militancy wastes. If a railroad is built, trade and intercourse indicate a line on which it ought to run; military strategy, however, overrules this and requires that it run otherwise. Then all the interests of trade and intercourse must be subjected to constant delay and expense because the line does not conform to them. Not a discovery or invention is made but the war and navy bureaus of all the great nations seize it to see what use can be made of it in war. It is evident that men love war; when two hundred thousand men in the United States volunteer in a month for a war with Spain which appeals to no sense of wrong against their country, and to no other strong sentiment of human nature, when their lives are by no means monotonous or destitute of interest, and where life offers chances of wealth and prosperity, the pure love of adventure and war must be strong in our population. Europeans who have to do military service have no such enthusiasm for war as war. The presence of such a sentiment in the midst of the most purely industrial state in the world is a wonderful phenomenon. At the same time the social philosophy of the modern civilized world is saturated with humanitarianism and flabby sentimentalism. The humanitarianism is in the literature; by it the reading public is led to suppose that the world is advancing along some line which they call "progress" towards peace and brotherly love. Nothing could be more mistaken. We read of fist-law and constant war in the Middle Ages and think that life must have been full of conflicts and bloodshed then; but modern warfare bears down on the whole population with a frightful weight through all the years of peace. Never, from the day of barbarism down to our own time, has every man in a society been a soldier until now; and the armaments of to-day are immensely more costly than ever before. There is only one limit possible to the war preparations of a modern European state; that is, the last man and the last dollar it can control. What will come of the mixture of sentimental social philosophy and warlike policy? There is only one thing rationally to be expected, and that is a frightful effusion of blood in revolution and war during the century now opening.

It is said that there are important offsets to all the burden and harm of this exaggerated militancy. That is true. Institutions and customs in human society are never either all good or all bad. We cannot adopt either peacefulness or warlikeness as a sole true philosophy. Military discipline educates; military interest awakens all the powers of men, so that they are eager to win and their ingenuity is quickened to invent new and better weapons. In history the military inventions have led the way and have been afterwards applied to industry. Chemical inventions were made in the attempt to produce combinations which would be destructive in war; we owe some of our most useful substances to discoveries which were made in this effort. The skill of artisans has been developed in making weapons, and then that skill has been available for industry. The only big machines which the ancients ever made were battering-rams, catapults, and other engines of war. The construction of these things familiarized men with mechanical devices which were capable of universal application. Gunpowder was discovered in the attempt to rediscover Greek fire; it was a grand invention in military art but we should never have had our canals, railroads, and other great works without such explosives. Again, we are indebted to the chemical experiments in search of military agents for our friction matches.

War also develops societal organization; it produces political institutions and classes. In the past these institutions and classes have been attended by oppression and by the exploitation of man by man; nevertheless, the more highly organized society has produced gains for all its members, including the oppressed or their posterity. The social exploitation is not essential to the organization, and it may be prevented by better provisions. In long periods of peace the whole societal structure becomes fixed in its adjustments and the functions all run into routine. Vested interests get an established control; some classes secure privileges and establish precedents, while other classes form habits of acquiescence. Traditions acquire a sacred character and philosophical doctrines are taught in churches and schools which make existing customs seem to be the "eternal order of nature." It becomes impossible to find a standing-ground from which to attack abuses and organize reform. Such was the case in France in the eighteenth century. By war new social powers break their way and create a new order. The student is tempted to think that even a great social convulsion is worth all it costs. What other force could break the bonds and open the way? But that is not the correct inference, because war and revolution never produce what is wanted, but only some mixture of the old evils with new ones; what is wanted is a peaceful and rational solution of problems and situations—but that requires great statesmanship and great popular sense and virtue. In the past the work has been done by war and revolution, with haphazard results and great attendant evils. To take an example from our own history: the banking and currency system of the United States, in 1860, was at a deadlock; we owe the national bank system, which was a grand reform of currency and banking, to the Civil War. It is impossible to see how else we could have overcome the vested interests and could have extricated ourselves from our position. It was no purpose of the war to reform the currency, but it gave an incidental opportunity and we had to win from it what we could.

There is another effect of war which is less obvious but more important. During a period of peace, rest, and routine, powers are developed which are in reality societal variations, among which a certain societal selection should take place. Here comes in the immense benefit of real liberty, because, if there is real liberty, a natural selection results; but if there is social prejudice, monopoly, privilege, orthodoxy, tradition, popular delusion, or any other restraint on liberty, selection does not occur. War operates a rude and imperfect selection. Our Civil War may serve as an example; think of the public men who were set aside by it and of the others who were brought forward by it, and compare them in character and ideas. Think of the doctrines which were set aside as false, and of the others which were established as true; also of the constitutional principles which were permanently stamped as heretical or orthodox. As a simple example, compare the position and authority of the President of the United States as it was before and as it has been since the Civil War. The Germans tell of the ruthless and cruel acts of Napoleon in Germany, and all that they say is true; but he did greater services to Germany than any other man who can be mentioned. He tore down the relics of mediævalism and set the powers of the nation to some extent free from the fetters of tradition; we do not see what else could have done it. It took another war in 1870 to root out the traditional institutions and make way for the new ones. Of course the whole national life responded to this selection. The Roman state was a selfish and pitiless subjugation of all the rest of mankind. It was built on slavery, it cost inconceivable blood and tears, and it was a grand system of extortion and plunder, but it gave security and peace under which the productive powers of the provinces expanded and grew. The Roman state gave discipline and organization and it devised institutions; the modern world has inherited societal elements from it which are invaluable. One of the silliest enthusiasms which ever got control of the minds of a great body of men was the Crusades, but the Crusades initiated a breaking up of the stagnation of the Dark Ages and an emancipation of· the social forces of Europe. They exerted a selective effect to destroy what was barbaric and deadening and to foster what had new hope in it by furnishing a stimulus to thought and knowledge.

A society needs to have a ferment in it; sometimes an enthusiastic delusion or an adventurous folly answers the purpose. In the modern world the ferment is furnished by economic opportunity and hope of luxury. In other ages it has often been furnished by war. Therefore some social philosophers have maintained that the best course of human affairs is an alternation of peace and war.[52] Some of them also argue that the only unity of the human race which can ever come about must be realized from the survival of the fittest in a war of weapons, in a conflict of usages, and in a rivalry issuing in adaptability to the industrial organization. It is not probable that aborigines will ever in the future be massacred in masses, as they have been in the past, but the case is even worse when, like our Indians for instance, they are set before a fatal dilemma. They cannot any longer live in their old way; they must learn to live by unskilled labor or by the mechanic arts. This, then, is the dilemma: to enter into the civilized industrial organization or to die out. If it had been possible for men to sit still in peace without civilization, they never would have achieved civilization; it is the iron spur of the nature-process which has forced them on, and one form of the

[52] Gumplowicz, L.: Grundriss der Sociologie, 125.

nature-process has been the attack of some men upon others who
were weaker than they.

We find, then, that in the past as a matter of fact war has
played a great part in the irrational nature-process by which
things have come to pass. But the nature-processes are frightful;
they contain no allowance for the feelings and interests of individuals—for it is only individuals who have feelings and interests. The nature-elements never suffer and they never pity. If we
are terrified at the nature-processes there is only one way to escape them; it is the way by which men have always evaded them
to some extent; it is by knowledge, by rational methods, and by
the arts. The facts which have been presented about the functions of war in the past are not flattering to the human reason
or conscience. They seem to show that we are as much indebted
for our welfare to base passion as to noble and intelligent endeavor. At the present moment things do not look much better.
We talk of civilizing lower races, but we never have done it yet;
we have exterminated them. Our devices for civilizing them have
been as disastrous to them as our firearms. At the beginning of
the twentieth century the great civilized nations are making
haste, in the utmost jealousy of each other, to seize upon all the
outlying parts of the globe; they are vying with each other in
the construction of navies by which each may defend its share
against the others. What will happen? As they are preparing for
war they certainly will have war, and their methods of coloniza-
tion and exploitation will destroy the aborigines. In this way the
human race will be civilized—but by the extermination of the
uncivilized—unless the men of the twentieth century can devise
plans for dealing with aborigines which are better than any
which have yet been devised. No one has yet found any way
in which two races, far apart in blood and culture, can be amal-
gamated into one society with satisfaction to both. Plainly, in
this matter which lies in the immediate future, the only alterna-
tives to force and bloodshed are more knowledge and more reason.

Shall any statesman, therefore, ever dare to say that it would
be well, at a given moment, to have a war, lest the nation fall

into the vices of industrialism and the evils of peace? The answer is plainly: No! War is never a handy remedy, which can be taken up and applied by routine rule. No war which can be avoided is just to the people who have to carry it on, to say nothing of the enemy. War is like other evils; it must be met when it is unavoidable, and such gain as can be got from it must be won. In the forum of reason and deliberation war never can be anything but a makeshift, to be regretted; it is the task of the statesman to find rational means to the same end. A statesman who proposes war as an instrumentality admits his incompetency; a politician who makes use of war as a counter in the game of parties is a criminal.

Can peace be universal? There is no reason to believe it. It is a fallacy to suppose that by widening the peace-group more and more it can at last embrace all mankind. What happens is that, as it grows bigger, differences, discords, antagonisms, and war begin inside of it on account of the divergence of interests. Since evil passions are a part of human nature and are in all societies all the time, a part of the energy of the society is constantly spent in repressing them. If all nations should resolve to have no armed ships any more, pirates would reappear upon the ocean; the police of the seas must be maintained. We could not dispense with our militia; we have too frequent need of it now. But police defense is not war in the sense in which I have been discussing it. War, in the future, will be the clash of policies of national vanity and selfishness when they cross each other's path.

If you want war, nourish a doctrine. Doctrines are the most frightful tyrants to which men ever are subject, because doctrines get inside of a man's own reason and betray him against himself. Civilized men have done their fiercest fighting for doctrines. The reconquest of the Holy Sepulcher, "the balance of power," "no universal dominion," "trade follows the flag," "he who holds the land will hold the sea," "the throne and the altar," the revolution, the faith—these are the things for which men have given their lives. What are they all? Nothing but rhetoric and phantasms. Doctrines are always vague; it would ruin a doctrine to define it, because then it could be analyzed, tested, criticised, and

verified; but nothing ought to be tolerated which cannot be so
tested. Somebody asks you with astonishment and horror whether
you do not believe in the Monroe Doctrine. You do not know
whether you do or not, because you do not know what it is; but
you do not dare to say that you do not, because you understand
that it is one of the things which every good American is bound
to believe in. Now when any doctrine arrives at that degree of
authority, the name of it is a club which any demagogue may
swing over you at any time and apropos of anything. In order
to describe a doctrine we must have recourse to theological language. A doctrine is an article of faith. It is something which
you are bound to believe, not because you have some rational
grounds for believing it true, but because you belong to such
and such a church or denomination. The nearest parallel to it
in politics is the "reason of state." The most frightful injustice
and cruelty which has ever been perpetrated on earth has been
due to the reason of state. Jesus Christ was put to death for the
reason of state; Pilate said that he found no fault in the ac-
cused, but he wanted to keep the Jews quiet and one man
crucified more or less was of no consequence. None of these
metaphysics ought to be tolerated in a free state. A policy in a
state we can understand; for instance it was the policy of the
United States at the end of the eighteenth century to get the
free navigation of the Mississippi to its mouth, even at the expense of war with Spain. That policy had reason and justice in
it; it was founded in our interests; it had positive form and
definite scope. A doctrine is an abstract principle; it is necessarily
absolute in its scope and abstruse in its terms; it is a metaphysical
assertion. It is never true, because it is absolute, and the affairs
of men are all conditioned and relative. The physicists tell us
now that there are phenomena which appear to present exceptions to gravitation which can be explained only by conceiving
that gravitation requires time to get to work. We are convinced
that perpetual motion is absolutely impossible within the world
of our experiences, but it now appears that our universe taken
as a whole is a case of perpetual motion.

Now, to turn back to politics, just think what an abomination
in statecraft an abstract doctrine must be. Any politician or

editor can, at any moment, put a new extension on it. The people acquiesce in the doctrine and applaud it because they hear the politicians and editors repeat it, and the politicians and editors repeat it because they think it is popular. So it grows. During the recent difficulty between England and Germany on one side and Venezuela on the other, some newspapers here began to promulgate a new doctrine that no country ought to be allowed to use its naval force to collect private debts. This doctrine would have given us standing-ground for interference in that quarrel. That is what it was invented for. Of course it was absurd and ridiculous, and it fell dead unnoticed, but it well showed the danger of having a doctrine lying loose about the house, and one which carries with it big consequences. It may mean anything or nothing, at any moment, and no one knows how it will be. You accede to it now, within the vague limits of what you suppose it to be; therefore you will have to accede to it to-morrow when the same name is made to cover something which you never have heard or thought of. If you allow a political catchword to go on and grow, you will awaken some day to find it standing over you, the arbiter of your destiny, against which you are powerless, as men are powerless against delusions.

The process by which such catchwords grow is the old popular mythologizing. Your Monroe Doctrine becomes an entity, a being, a lesser kind of divinity, entitled to reverence and possessed of prestige, so that it allows of no discussion or deliberation. The President of the United States talks about the Monroe Doctrine and he tells us solemnly that it is true and sacred, whatever it is. He even undertakes to give some definition of what he means by it; but the definition which he gives binds nobody, either now or in the future, any more than what Monroe and Adams meant by it binds anybody now not to mean anything else. He says that, on account of the doctrine, whatever it may be, we must have a big navy. In this, at least, he is plainly in the right; if we have the doctrine, we shall need a big navy. The Monroe Doctrine is an exercise of authority by the United States over a controversy between two foreign states, if one of them is in America, combined with a refusal of the United States to accept any responsibility in connection with the controversy. That is a position which is sure to bring us into collision with other States, especially because it will touch their vanity, or what they call their honor—or it will touch our vanity, or what we call our honor, if we should ever find ourselves called upon to "back down" from it. Therefore it is very true that we must expect to need a big navy if we adhere to the doctrine. What can be more contrary to sound statesmanship and common sense than to put forth an abstract assertion which has no definite relation to any interest of ours now at stake, but which has in it any number of possibilities of producing complications which we cannot foresee, but which are sure to be embarrassing when they arise!

(What has just been said suggests a consideration of the popular saying, "In time of peace prepare for war." If you prepare a big army and navy and are all ready for war, it will be easy to go to war; the military and naval men will have a lot of new machines and they will be eager to see what they can do with them.) There is no such thing nowadays as a state of readiness for war. It is a chimera, and the nations which pursue it are falling into an abyss of wasted energy and wealth. When the army is supplied with the latest and best rifles, someone invents a new field gun; then the artillery must be provided with that before we are ready. By the time we get the new gun, somebody has invented a new rifle and our rival nation is getting that; therefore we must have it, or one a little better. It takes two or three years and several millions to do that. In the meantime somebody proposes a more effective organization which must be introduced, signals, balloons, dogs, bicycles, and every other device and invention must be added, and men must be trained to use them all. There is no state of readiness for war; the notion calls for never-ending sacrifices. It is a fallacy. It is evident that to pursue such a notion with any idea of realizing it would absorb all the resources and activity of the state; this the great European states are now proving by experiment. A wiser rule would be to make up your mind soberly what you want, peace or war, and then to get ready for what you want; for what we prepare for is what we shall get.

III

Social War in Democracy

It is one of those popular assumptions of our time which, although never distinctly formulated, have such an important part in all our accepted faiths, that social forces change in the progress of civilization, so that, for example, slavery and feudalism pass away completely. The students of social history, however, find that social forces are ever the same; only the phenomena present themselves under new combinations. It is when this fact forces itself upon the observation of men in spite of their pet dogmas, that we hear about the "labor problem," or "wage slavery." Men toss and heave and squirm, changing their position from generation to generation; they have always just got, or are about just to get, the final and completely satisfactory solution, and they find that the hardships of life, the difficulty of getting a living, the task of rearing children, pain, disease, and death, remain about the same. The new discovery, instead of annihilating ills and closing the account of earthly hardship, proves only the point of departure for new ills unknown before; and the old ills brighten as they take their flight, for their unappreciated advantages come to light.

Let us notice how class struggles have run through modern history and see what the position of democracy is in respect to class struggles and social war.

The feudal system properly had only two classes, nobles and peasants; kings were differentiated from nobles and they made a breach in the system.) In Russia and Poland these three classes fought it out, and the difference in the results has a value for the student of political class struggles which no one has yet, to my knowledge, developed. In Russia the crown won; the nobles never became "nobles" in the Western sense; the peasants were reduced to serfdom as mere pawns in the game. They always maintained a tradition that the Czar had subjected them to servitude under the nobles that the latter might fight for the fatherland—a capital instance of what comes of sacrificing private rights to "the greater good of the state." In Poland the crown was subjugated to the nobles, and then the latter developed a tyranny over the peasants far worse than that of Russia, and reduced their country first to anarchy and then to foreign conquest.

In Western Europe another class was differentiated from the two classes of feudalism—the middle class, the *bourgeoisie* of the cities. This made four classes, and political history has been moulded by their alliances and conflicts. The middle class was at war with feudalism; while the lords were strong the monarchs and cities combined against them. In Germany the crown could not win a real victory, while in France and Spain it did do so. In England the four classes came to a compromise and adjustment under the Constitution, but their rubbing against each other has marked the history of that country for five hundred years.

(Now, if we have a democratic republic, the crown disappears out of it. If the economic situation is that of a new country, with sparse population and an abundance of land, there are no nobles, and in an older country, under the democratic republican form, there cease to be any nobles. Titles are a mere matter of courtesy and have only social value.) There remain then only two classes, the *bourgeoisie* and the peasantry, and these undergo very important modifications. The high *bourgeoisie* develops into a class of wealth and luxury, supplanting, imitating, reproducing with variations, the old baronage; it struggles to form out of itself a patriciate—a body of selected families defined by its own sympathies and voluntary recognition, or a body of locupletes or optimates, or a timocracy of those who have enjoyed the honors of the state. The process has been repeated so often in the classical states, in the Italian republics, and in the rich cities of the Middle Ages that it ought to be sufficiently familiar to us. The force at work is plainly the trait of human nature which leads men to gratify their vanity, to seek to excel, to try to guarantee the future of their children, and to secure the fruits of their own efforts. Like all other traits of human nature, it has its good side and its bad side.

On the other hand the modern representatives of the ancient peasantry are very different from their predecessors. The middle class is constantly fed from them at the bottom. A class of yeomen farmers or peasant proprietors has little in common in its status, its fund of ideas, or its outlook, with mediæval peasants. There are no peasants in the modern Western world with whom the other classes can play, or whom they can afford to disregard.

In this matter also the modern statesman is all ready to act. The chip which floated on the current thought that it made the river go; so statesmen and political philosophers think that they make institutions and mould history. The thing which makes and breaks institutions is economic forces, acting on the interests of men, and, through them, on human nature. The statesman who goes along with these forces, wins great "triumphs"; but he is like the chip on the current, after all; the most that he does is to show in which direction it is going. Now the cheapening of transportation between the great centers of population and the great outlying masses of unoccupied land is the greatest fact of our time, and it is the greatest economic and social revolution which has ever taken place. We, of this generation, are the first ones to see the real effects of the discovery of America beginning to operate on the whole social system of the Old World. Through the reduction in the rent of land there, the present forces are undermining and will presently sweep away the whole class system built upon the competition of a dense population for a limited area of land. The fall in rent, the obliteration of social distinctions, the decline of aristocracy, the rise of democracy, the subdivision of great estates, the rise of peasant proprietors, are all consequences of the economic revolution—consequences which no statesman or philosopher has made or can prevent;

but there will, no doubt, be a great number of conventions held and innumerable "resolutions" will be passed "approving" of the change, and thereby claiming to have caused it; and the world will be enriched by a number of great statesmen who will be credited with having made it all.

A land-owning peasant class and a property-owning middle class do not appear likely to go to war with each other. On the contrary, the social combinations which must arise under the new order of things are already discernible: it is plainly the antagonism of those-who-have and those-who-have-not which is to rise out of the social residuum, when kings and nobles and old-fashioned peasants are gone; and the middle class, covering a wider compass between its extremes, is left alone. It is then that the test of democracy and of the current political philosophy must come. With a proud and powerful plutocracy on one side, and a hungry proletariat on the other, can democracy find resources anywhere for controlling the elements of human greed and passion? A plutocracy wants to obtain free swing for its powers through and over the social organization. It wants, above all, security and guarantees for what-is, for what-has-been-accomplished for capital and accumulated wealth. The proletariat wants free swing for the forces of new creation, for what-is-to-be, for the unaccomplished. The former wants quiet enjoyment, the latter wants free chance for enterprise.

It is an easy thing, now, to get a majority to vote that the capital-which-is belongs to the chances of the new effort for what-is-to-be, and to resolve accordingly that those-who-have-not, belonging to the party of enterprise and of the future, ought to, and of right must take possession of the capital now "detained" by the party of the past and of the thing-accomplished, in order to go on with progress. We have already had an abundance of philosophers profound enough to prophesy this unto us; but when these notions turn from the precepts of philosophers into the program of parties under a democracy, we see that the old social war is not over. It is not settled: the old evils are not abolished; the passions are not stifled—they are all here under new forms. The robbery of a merchant by a robber baron, the robbery of an investor by a railroad wrecker, and the robbery of a capitalist by a collectivist, are all one. Democracy as a political form, instead of settling anything, has set them all loose; what, now, should be and can be its policy toward them? If it stands away from them, only insisting on peace and order and upon submission by everybody to the administration of rights according to contract, then the landlord who finds that his rents fall, or the railroad investor who gets no dividends, or the producer who is dissatisfied with the price which his product brings, will have no recourse except each against himself. He will have to learn more, and to become wiser. Inasmuch as this would call reason and conscience into play, there might really be some hope that we might gain something toward doing away with social war; but that democracy can solve the antagonisms in the newest order of things, can adjust the rights of the contending interests by a series of "ethical" decisions, or that it can, by siding with one party, give it a victory over the other, and thereby found a stable social order, it is folly to believe.

IV

Some Natural Rights

The mediæval notion about rights was that they were franchises or grants from the head of the state; each man started with just such ones, and so many of them as his ancestors had succeeded in getting out of the struggle of war and court intrigue. If his ancestors had not been successful in that struggle, he had none. The theoretical basis of the civil system was, therefore, the assumption that, in advance of action by the civil authority, man as such had no rights. All must be assumed to be under the same constraints and restrictions, until, by franchises, privileges, and exemptions, each of which was capable of proof by legal evidence, documents, or tradition, some had emancipated themselves from the restrictions. As these franchises and privileges admitted of every variety, when compared with each other or combined with each other, there could be no equality. In the system, the fact that one man had obtained a certain charter was no reason why anybody else should have the same.

It will be found again and again in examining the political and social dogmas which were enunciated in the eighteenth century, and which have become commonplaces and catchwords in the nineteenth, that they had their origin in a just and true revolt against the doctrines of mediæval society, so that they are intelligible and valuable, when viewed in their historical connection, however doubtful they may be when taken as universal *a priori* dogmas.

In the case just stated, we have an instance of this. The eighteenth-century notion of "natural rights," or of the "rights of man," was a revolt against the notion that a man had nothing and was entitled to nothing until some other men had given him some rights here. The rights of man meant that a man, as a man, entered human society, not under servitude and constraint to other men, or to social traditions, but under a presumption of non-servitude and non-obligation to other men, or to social organization. Natural rights, as opposed to chartered rights, meant that the fundamental presumption must be changed, and that every man must, in the view of social order and obligation, be regarded as free and independent, until some necessity had been established for restraining him, instead of being held to be in complete subjection to social bonds, until he could prove that some established authority had emancipated him.

When so regarded, it is evident that the notion of natural rights is one of great value and importance. In the abuse of it, however, it has come to pass that this notion has become a doctrine which affords the most ample space for arbitrary dogmatism, and empty declamation. It has become one of the favorite methods of modern schemers, when they find it difficult to provide means by which men may get what they need in order to enjoy earthly comfort, to put all those necessary things among "natural rights." It then stands established, by easy deduction, that every man has a natural right to succeed in the struggle for existence, or to be happy. It is the duty of the state to secure natural rights. Therefore, if there is anything which a man wants, he is entitled to have it so long as there is any of it.

The notion that all men are equal is likewise reasonable and useful when taken in its historical setting. It meant, in contradiction to the mediæval notion, that whatever rights the state might give to some, it should give to all, and that whatever burdens it laid on some, it should lay on all, without distinction of persons or classes. No such thing has ever been realized or ever can be, and the doctrine would need modification and limitation to make it true, but, as a revolt against mediævalism, it is intelligible. In its best form it is our modern "equality before the law"; but we are constantly striving to use the state to give privileges, and then to make the privileges equal, or to give them to everybody. Turn all such propositions as we will, they are only attempts to lift ourselves by our boot-straps, or to bring good things into existence by decree.

Ever since it has been accepted doctrine that there are natural rights, innumerable attempts have been made to formulate "declarations" of them, that is, to tell what they are. No such attempt has ever succeeded, and the history of the effort to define and specify what the rights of man are is instructive for the sense and value of the notion itself. At present this effort is prosecuted, not by parliaments and conventions, but by social philosophers. As these attempts go on, they develop more and more completely the futility of the notion, or its purely mischievous character as a delusion which draws us away from what might profit us.

Among the latest enunciations of the fundamental and universal rights of man, is that of "the right to the full product of labor." This has been declared, in the most intelligent exposition of it known to me,[1] to be the same as "the right to an existence." The two "rights" are in plain contradiction.

In the first place, the "right to the complete product of labor" contains one of the usual ambiguities. Is it meant that the man who does any manual labor in connection with, or contribution to the production of a thing, should have the whole of that thing? Or, is it meant that the man who contributes manual labor to the productive enterprise should have all that part of the thing which belongs to the labor element, in proportion to the capital, land, and other elements which contribute to production? If the former, then we are face to face with a proposition for robbery, with all the social consequences which must be anticipated. Furthermore, although it may seem a very simple thing to provide that those who do the manual work shall have all the product, it is plain, so soon as we reflect upon the complicated combinations of labor which are involved in any case of production, and also upon the complicated character of modern "products" and the way in which they contribute to, and depend

[1] A. Menger, "Das Recht auf den vollen Arbeitsertrag." Stuttgart, 1886.

upon each other, that it would be impracticable to divide the products among those who have done the labor part of production.

If it is meant that the labor element shall have all the part of the product which is due to the labor element in it, the question arises, how is that element to be measured? How is its proportion to the whole to be determined? At present it is done by supply and demand, and until we have some standard of measurement provided, we cannot tell whether the present arrangement does not do just what is desired. There are constantly reiterated assertions that it does not. It is well worth noticing that no ground for these assertions is offered, and that there is no possibility of verifying them unless some standard of measurement can be proposed by which we can find out what the share ought to be, and compare it with what is.

In any case the right to the full product of labor would be contradictory to the right to an existence, for, if the full product of the labor of some falls short of what is necessary to maintain their existence, then they must encroach upon the full labor product of the others, that is, impair the right of the latter. The "right to an existence," however, has the advantage of putting the notion in a distinct and complete form; it covers the whole ground at once; it no longer spends energy in struggling for such means as the right to property, or labor, or liberty, or life. If dogmatic affirmation can do anything, why waste it on the means? Why not expend it at once upon the desired end? The real misery of mankind is the struggle for existence; why not "declare" that there ought not to be any struggle for existence, and that there shall not be any more? Let it be decreed that existence is a natural right, and let it be secured in that way.

If we attempt to execute this plan, it is plain that we shall not abolish the struggle for existence; we shall only bring it about that some men must fight that struggle for others.

Although the right of existence has the advantage of being broad and radical, it has the disadvantage of being abstract and impracticable. Another writer[2] has recently given another formula, which, although less ambitious, is equally effective and

[2] "Le Droit au Capital, par Le Solitaire." Paris, 1886.

far more practical; he affirms the natural right to capital. This must be regarded as the rational outcome, so far, of the attempt to formulate natural rights. All the good things which we want, and find so hard to get, depend on capital. Logically, it is less satisfactory to demand a means than to demand an end; but when the means is the one complete and only necessary one, that point is of little importance. If we could all have capital, we should have the great and only weapon for the struggle for existence. It is only a pity, however, that, in this case, as in all the others, so soon as we get a good formula, it turns out to be either a contradiction, a bathos, an impracticability, or an absurdity. So long as capital has to be brought into existence by human labor and self-denial, if we set up a right to capital in all men, we shall have to affirm that those who have not produced the capital have a right to have it, but that those who have produced it have not a right to have it, since from these latter we take it away.

V

Socialism[1]

Socialism is no new thing. In one form or another it is to be found throughout all history. It arises from an observation of certain harsh facts in the lot of man on earth, the concrete expression of which is poverty and misery. These facts challenge us. It is folly to try to shut our eyes to them. We have first to notice what they are, and then to face them squarely.

Man is born under the necessity of sustaining the existence he has received by an onerous struggle against nature, both to win what is essential to his life and to ward off what is prejudicial to it. He is born under a burden and a necessity. Nature holds what is essential to him, but she offers nothing gratuitously. He may win for his use what she holds, if he can. Only the most meager and inadequate supply for human needs can be obtained directly from nature. There are trees which may be used for fuel and for dwellings, but labor is required to fit them for this use. There are ores in the ground, but labor is necessary to get out the metals and make tools or weapons. For any real satisfaction, labor is necessary to fit the products of nature for human use. In this struggle every individual is under the pressure of the necessities for food, clothing, shelter, fuel, and every individual brings with him more or less energy for the conflict necessary to supply his needs. The relation, therefore, between each man's needs and

[1] A. G. Keller, Sumner's student and the editor of his collected papers, entitled this essay "The Challenge of Facts." Sumner's own title is here restored.—[S. P.]

each man's energy, or "individualism," is the first fact of human life.

It is not without reason, however, that we speak of a "man" as the individual in question, for women (mothers) and children have special disabilities for the struggle with nature, and these disabilities grow greater and last longer as civilization advances. The perpetuation of the race in health and vigor, and its success as a whole in its struggle to expand and develop human life on earth, therefore, require that the head of the family shall, by his energy, be able to supply not only his own needs, but those of the organisms which are dependent upon him. The history of the human race shows a great variety of experiments in the relation of the sexes and in the organization of the family. These experiments have been controlled by economic circumstances, but, as man has gained more and more control over economic circumstances, monogamy and the family education of children have been more and more sharply developed. If there is one thing in regard to which the student of history and sociology can affirm with confidence that social institutions have made progress" or grown "better," it is in this arrangement of marriage and the family. All experience proves that monogamy, pure and strict, is the sex relation which conduces most to the vigor and intelligence of the race, and that the family education of children is the institution by which the race as a whole advances most rapidly, from generation to generation, in the struggle with nature. Love of man and wife, as we understand it, is a modern sentiment. The devotion and sacrifice of parents for children is a sentiment which has been developed steadily and is now more intense and far more widely practiced throughout society than in earlier times. The relation is also coming to be regarded in a light quite different from that in which it was formerly viewed. It used to be believed that the parent had unlimited claims on the child and rights over him. In a truer view of the matter, we are coming to see that the rights are on the side of the child and the duties on the side of the parent. Existence is not a boon for which the child owes all subjection to the parent. It is a responsibility assumed by the parent towards the child without the child's consent, and the consequence of it is that the parent owes all possible devotion to the child to enable him to make his existence happy and successful.

The value and importance of the family sentiments, from a social point of view, cannot be exaggerated. They impose self-control and prudence in their most important social bearings, and tend more than any other forces to hold the individual up to the virtues which make the sound man and the valuable member of society. The race is bound, from generation to generation, in an unbroken chain of vice and penalty, virtue and reward. The sins of the fathers are visited upon the children, while, on the other hand, health, vigor, talent, genius, and skill are, so far as we can discover, the results of high physical vigor and wise early training. The popular language bears witness to the universal observation of these facts, although general social and political dogmas have come into fashion which contradict or ignore them. There is no other such punishment for a life of vice and self-indulgence as to see children grow up cursed with the penalties of it, and no such reward for self-denial and virtue as to see children born and grow up vigorous in mind and body. It is time that the true import of these observations for moral and educational purposes was developed, and it may well be questioned whether we do not go too far in our reticence in regard to all these matters when we leave it to romances and poems to do almost all the educational work that is done in the way of spreading ideas about them. The defense of marriage and the family, if their sociological value were better understood, would be not only instinctive but rational. The struggle for existence with which we have to deal must be understood, then, to be that of a man for himself, his wife, and his children.

The next great fact we have to notice in regard to the struggle of human life is that labor which is spent in a direct struggle with nature is severe in the extreme and is but slightly productive. To subjugate nature, man needs weapons and tools. These, however, cannot be won unless the food and clothing and other prime and direct necessities are supplied in such amount that they can be consumed while tools and weapons are being made, for the tools and weapons themselves satisfy no needs directly. A man who tills the ground with his fingers or with a pointed stick picked up without labor will get a small crop. To fashion even the rudest spade or hoe will cost time, during which the laborer must still eat and drink and wear, but the tool, when obtained, will multiply immensely the power to produce. Such products of labor, used to assist production, have a function so peculiar in the nature of things that we need to distinguish them. We call them capital. A lever is capital, and the advantage of lifting a weight with a lever over lifting it by direct exertion is only a feeble illustration of the power of capital in production. The origin of capital lies in the darkness before history, and it is probably impossible for us to imagine the slow and painful steps by which the race began the formation of it. Since then it has gone on rising to higher and higher powers by a ceaseless involution, if I may use a mathematical expression. Capital is labor raised to a higher power by being constantly multiplied into itself. Nature has been more and more subjugated by the human race through the power of capital, and every human being now living shares the improved status of the race to a degree which neither he nor any one else can measure, and for which he pays nothing.

Let us understand this point, because our subject will require future reference to it. It is the most short-sighted ignorance not to see that, in a civilized community, all the advantage of capital except a small fraction is gratuitously enjoyed by the community. For instance, suppose the case of a man utterly destitute of tools, who is trying to till the ground with a pointed stick. He could get something out of it. If now he should obtain a spade with which to till the ground, let us suppose, for illustration, that he could get twenty times as great a product. Could, then, the owner of a spade in a civilized state demand, as its price, from the man who had no spade, nineteen-twentieths of the product which could be produced by the use of it? Certainly not. The price of a spade is fixed by the supply and demand of products in the community. A spade is bought for a dollar and the gain from the use of it is an inheritance of knowledge, experience, and skill which every man who lives in a civilized state gets for nothing. What we pay for steam transportation is no trifle, but imagine, if you can, eastern Massachusetts cut off from steam connection with the rest of the world, turnpikes and sailing vessels remaining. The cost of food would rise so high that a quarter of the population would starve to death and another quarter would have to emigrate. To-day every man here gets an enormous advantage from the status of a society on a level of steam transportation, telegraph, and machinery, for which he pays nothing.

So far as I have yet spoken, we have before us the struggle of man with nature, but the social problems, strictly speaking, arise at the next step. Each man carries on the struggle to win his support for himself, but there are others by his side engaged in the same struggle. If the stores of nature were unlimited, or if the last unit of the supply she offers could be won as easily as the first, there would be no social problem. If a square mile of land could support an indefinite number of human beings, or if it cost only twice as much labor to get forty bushels of wheat from an acre as to get twenty, we should have no social problem. If a square mile of land could support millions, no one would ever emigrate and there would be no trade or commerce. If it cost only twice as much labor to get forty bushels as twenty, there would be no advance in the arts. The fact is far otherwise. So long as the population is low in proportion to the amount of land, on a given stage of the arts, life is easy and the competition of man with man is weak. When more persons are trying to live on a square mile than it can support, on the existing stage of the arts, life is hard and the competition of man with man is intense. In the former case, industry and prudence may be on a low grade; the penalties are not severe, or certain, or speedy. In the latter case, each individual needs to exert on his own behalf every force, original or acquired, which he can command. In the former case, the average condition will be one of comfort and the population will be all nearly on the average. In the latter case, the average condition will not be one of comfort, but the population will cover wide extremes of comfort and misery. Each will find his place according to his ability and his effort. The former society will be democratic; the latter will be aristocratic.

The constant tendency of population to outstrip the means of

subsistence is the force which has distributed population over
the world, and produced all advance in civilization. To this day
the two means of escape for an overpopulated country are emigration and an advance in the arts. The former wins more land
for the same people; the latter makes the same land support more
persons. If, however, either of these means opens a chance for
an increase of population, it is evident that the advantage so
won may be speedily exhausted if the increase takes place. The
social difficulty has only undergone a temporary amelioration,
and when the conditions of pressure and competition are re-
newed, misery and poverty reappear. The victims of them are
those who have inherited disease and depraved appetites, or have
been brought up in vice and ignorance, or have themselves
yielded to vice, extravagance, idleness, and imprudence. In the
last analysis, therefore, we come back to vice, in its original and
hereditary forms, as the correlative of misery and poverty.

The condition for the complete and regular action of the force
of competition is liberty. Liberty means the security given to each
man that, if he employs his energies to sustain the struggle on
behalf of himself and those he cares for, he shall dispose of the
product exclusively as he chooses. It is impossible to know
whence any definition or criterion of justice can be derived, if
it is not deduced from this view of things; or if it is not the
definition of justice that each shall enjoy the fruit of his own
labor and self-denial, and of injustice that the idle and the industrious, the self-indulgent and the self-denying, shall share
equally in the product. Aside from the *a priori* speculations of
philosophers who have tried to make equality an essential element in justice, the human race has recognized, from the earliest
times, the above conception of justice as the true one, and has
founded upon it the right of property. The right of property,
with marriage and the family, gives the right of bequest.

Monogamic marriage, however, is the most exclusive of social
institutions. It contains, as essential principles, preference, superiority, selection, devotion. It would not be at all what it is if it
were not for these characteristic traits, and it always degenerates
when these traits are not present. For instance, if a man should
not have a distinct preference for the woman he married, and if

he did not select her as superior to others, the marriage would be an imperfect one according to the standard of true monogamic marriage. The family under monogamy, also, is a closed group, having special interests and estimating privacy and reserve as valuable advantages for family development. We grant high prerogatives, in our society, to parents, although our observation teaches us that thousands of human beings are unfit to be parents or to be entrusted with the care of children. It follows, therefore, from the organization of marriage and the family, under monogamy, that great inequalities must exist in a society based on those institutions. The son of wise parents cannot start on a level with the son of foolish ones, and the man who has had no home discipline cannot be equal to the man who has had home discipline. If the contrary were true, we could rid ourselves at once of the wearing labor of inculcating sound morals and manners in our children.

Private property, also, which we have seen to be a feature of society organized in accordance with the natural conditions of the struggle for existence produces inequalities between men. The struggle for existence is aimed against nature. It is from her niggardly hand that we have to wrest the satisfactions for our needs, but our fellow-men are our competitors for the meager supply. Competition, therefore, is a law of nature. Nature is entirely neutral; she submits to him who most energetically and resolutely assails her. She grants her rewards to the fittest, therefore, without regard to other considerations of any kind. If, then, there be liberty, men get from her just in proportion to their works, and their having and enjoying are just in proportion to their being and their doing. Such is the system of nature. If we do not like it, and if we try to amend it, there is only one way in which we can do it. We can take from the better and give to the worse. We can deflect the penalties of those who have done ill and throw them on those who have done better. We can take the rewards from those who have done better and give them to those who have done worse. We shall thus lessen the inequalities. We shall favor the survival of the unfittest, and we shall accomplish this by destroying liberty. Let it be understood that we cannot go outside of this alternative: liberty, inequality, survival of the fittest; not-liberty, equality, survival of the unfittest. The former carries society forward and favors all its best members; the latter carries society downwards and favors all its worst members.

For three hundred years now men have been trying to understand and realize liberty. Liberty is not the right or chance to do what we choose; there is no such liberty as that on earth. No man can do as he chooses: the autocrat of Russia or the King of Dahomey has limits to his arbitrary will; the savage in the wilderness, whom some people think free, is the slave of routine, tradition, and superstitious fears; the civilized man must earn his living, or take care of his property, or concede his own will to the rights and claims of his parents, his wife, his children, and all the persons with whom he is connected by the ties and contracts of civilized life.

What we mean by liberty is civil liberty, or liberty under law; and this means the guarantees of law that a man shall not be interfered with while using his own powers for his own welfare. It is, therefore, a civil and political status; and that nation has the freest institutions in which the guarantees of peace for the laborer and security for the capitalist are the highest. Liberty, therefore, does not by any means do away with the struggle for existence. We might as well try to do away with the need of eating, for that would, in effect, be the same thing. What civil liberty does is to turn the competition of man with man from violence and brute force into an industrial competition under which men vie with one another for the acquisition of material goods by industry, energy, skill, frugality, prudence, temperance, and other industrial virtues. Under this changed order of things the inequalities are not done away with. Nature still grants her rewards of having and enjoying, according to our being and doing, but it is now the man of the highest training and not the man of the heaviest fist who gains the highest reward. It is impossible that the man with capital and the man without capital should be equal. To affirm that they are equal would be to say that a man who has no tool can get as much food out of the ground as the man who has a spade or a plough; or that the man who has no weapon can defend himself as well against hostile beasts or hostile men as the man who has a weapon. If that were so, none of us would work any more. We work and deny ourselves to get capital just because, other things being equal, the man who has it is superior, for attaining all the ends of life, to the man who has it not. Considering the eagerness with which we all seek capital and the estimate we put upon it, either in cherishing it if we have it, or envying others who have it while we have it not, it is very strange what platitudes pass current about it in our society so soon as we begin to generalize about it. If our young people really believed some of the teachings they hear, it would not be amiss to preach them a sermon once in a while to reassure them, setting forth that it is not wicked to be rich, nay even, that it is not wicked to be richer than your neighbor.

It follows from what we have observed that it is the utmost folly to denounce capital. To do so is to undermine civilization, for capital is the first requisite of every social gain, educational, ecclesiastical, political, æsthetic, or other.

It must also be noticed that the popular antithesis between persons and capital is very fallacious. Every law or institution which protects persons at the expense of capital makes it easier for persons to live and to increase the number of consumers of capital while lowering all the motives to prudence and frugality by which capital is created. Hence every such law or institution tends to produce a large population, sunk in misery. All poor laws and all eleemosynary institutions and expenditures have this tendency. On the contrary, all laws and institutions which give security to capital against the interests of other persons than its owners, restrict numbers while preserving the means of subsistence. Hence every such law or institution tends to produce a small society on a high stage of comfort and well-being. It follows that the antithesis commonly thought to exist between the protection of persons and the protection of property is in reality only an antithesis between numbers and quality.

I must stop to notice, in passing, one other fallacy which is rather scientific than popular. The notion is attributed to certain economists that economic forces are self-correcting. I do not know of any economists who hold this view, but what is intended probably is that many economists, of whom I venture to be one, hold that economic forces act compensatingly, and that whenever economic forces have so acted as to produce an unfavorable situation, other economic forces are brought into action which correct the evil and restore the equilibrium. For instance, in Ireland overpopulation and exclusive devotion to agriculture, both of which are plainly traceable to unwise statesmanship in the past, have produced a situation of distress. Steam navigation on the ocean has introduced the competition of cheaper land with Irish agriculture. The result is a social and industrial crisis. There are, however, millions of acres of fertile land on earth which are unoccupied and which are open to the Irish, and the economic forces are compelling the direct corrective of the old evils, in the way of emigration or recourse to urban occupations by unskilled labor. Any number of economic and legal nostrums have been proposed for this situation, all of which propose to leave the original causes untouched. We are told that economic causes do not correct themselves. That is true. We are told that when an economic situation becomes very grave it goes on from worse to worse and that there is no cycle through which it returns. That is not true, without further limitation. We are told that moral forces alone can elevate any such people again. But it is plain that a people which has sunk below the reach of the economic forces of self-interest has certainly sunk below the reach of moral forces, and that this objection is superficial and short-sighted. What is true is that economic forces always go before moral forces. Men feel self-interest long before they feel prudence, self-control, and temperance. They lose the moral forces long before they lose the economic forces. If they can be regenerated at all, it must be first by distress appealing to self-interest and forcing recourse to some expedient for relief. Emigration is certainly an economic force for the relief of Irish distress. It is a palliative only, when considered in itself, but the virtue of it is that it gives the non-emigrating population a chance to rise to a level on which the moral forces can act upon them. Now it is terribly true that only the better ones emigrate, and only the better ones among those who remain are capable of having their ambition and energy awakened, but for the rest the solution is famine and death, with a social regeneration through decay and the elimination of that part of the society which is not capable of being restored to health and life. As Mr. Huxley[2] once said, the method of nature is not even a word and a blow, with the blow first. No explanation is vouchsafed. We are left to find out for ourselves why our ears are boxed. If we do not find out, and find out correctly, what the error is for which we are being punished, the blow is repeated and poverty, distress, disease, and death finally remove the incorrigible ones. It behooves us men to study these terrible illustrations of the penalties which follows on bad statesmanship, and of the sanctions by which social laws are enforced. The economic cycle does complete itself; it must do so, unless the social group is to sink in permanent barbarism. A law may be passed which shall force somebody to support the hopelessly degenerate members of a society, but such a law can only perpetuate the evil and entail it on future generations with new accumulations of distress.

The economic forces work with moral forces and are their handmaidens, but the economic forces are far more primitive, original, and universal. The glib generalities in which we sometimes hear people talk, as if you could set moral and economic forces separate from and in antithesis to each other, and discard the one to accept and work by the other, gravely misconstrue the realities of the social order.

We have now before us the facts of human life out of which the social problem springs. These facts are in many respects hard and stern. It is by strenuous exertion only that each one of us can sustain himself against the destructive forces and the ever recurring needs of life; and the higher the degree to which we seek to carry our development the greater is the proportionate cost of every step. For help in the struggle we can only look back to those in the previous generation who are responsible for our existence. In the competition of life the son of wise and prudent ancestors has immense advantages over the son of vicious and imprudent ones. The man who has capital possesses immeasurable advantages for the struggle of life over him who has none. The more we break down privileges of class, or industry,

[2] Thomas Henry Huxley (1825-1895), British naturalist. [S. P.]

and establish liberty, the greater will be the inequalities and the more exclusively will the vicious bear the penalties. Poverty and misery will exist in society just so long as vice exists in human nature.

I now go on to notice some modes of trying to deal with this problem. There is a modern philosophy which has never been taught systematically, but which has won the faith of vast masses of people in the modern civilized world. For want of a better name it may be called the sentimental philosophy. It has colored all modern ideas and institutions in politics, religion, education, charity, and industry, and is widely taught in popular literature, novels, and poetry, and in the pulpit. The first proposition of this sentimental philosophy is that nothing is true which is disagreeable. If, therefore, any facts of observation show that life is grim or hard, the sentimental philosophy steps over such facts with a genial platitude, a consoling commonplace, or a gratifying dogma. The effect is to spread an easy optimism, under the influence of which people spare themselves labor and trouble, reflection and forethought, pains and caution—all of which are hard things, and to admit the necessity for which would be to admit that the world is not all made smooth and easy, for us to pass through it surrounded by love, music, and flowers.

Under this philosophy, "progress" has been represented as a steadily increasing and unmixed good; as if the good steadily encroached on the evil without involving any new and other forms of evil; and as if we could plan great steps in progress in our academies and lyceums, and then realize them by resolution. To minds trained to this way of looking at things, any evil which exists is a reproach. We have only to consider it, hold some discussions about it, pass resolutions, and have done with it. Every moment of delay is, therefore, a social crime. It is monstrous to say that misery and poverty are as constant as vice and evil passions of men! People suffer so under misery and poverty! Assuming, therefore, that we can solve all these problems and eradicate all these evils by expending our ingenuity upon them, of course we cannot hasten too soon to do it.

A social philosophy, consonant with this, has also been taught for a century. It could not fail to be popular, for it teaches that

ignorance is as good as knowledge, vulgarity as good as refinement, shiftlessness as good as painstaking, shirking as good as
faithful striving, poverty as good as wealth, filth as good as
cleanliness—in short, that quality goes for nothing in the
measurement of men, but only numbers. Culture, knowledge,
refinement, skill, and taste cost labor, but we have been taught
that they have only individual, not social value, and that socially
they are rather drawbacks than otherwise. In public life we are
taught to admire roughness, illiteracy, and rowdyism. The ignorant, idle, and shiftless have been taught that they are "the
people," that the generalities inculcated at the same time about
the dignity, wisdom, and virtue of "the people" are true of them,
that they have nothing to learn to be wise, but that, as they stand,
they possess a kind of infallibility, and that to their "opinion"
the wise must bow. It is not cause for wonder if whole sections
of these classes have begun to use the powers and wisdom attributed to them for their interests, as they construe them, and to
trample on all the excellence which marks civilization as on
obsolete superstition.

Another development of the same philosophy is the doctrine
that men come into the world endowed with "natural rights,"
or as joint inheritors of the "rights of man," which have been
"declared" times without number during the last century. The
divine rights of man have succeeded to the obsolete divine right
of kings. If it is true, then, that a man is born with rights, he
comes into the world with claims on somebody besides his
parents. Against whom does he hold such rights? There can be
no rights against nature or against God. A man may curse his
fate because he is born of an inferior race, or with an hereditary
disease, or blind, or, as some members of the race seem to do,
because they are born females; but they get no answer to their
imprecations. But, now, if men have rights by birth, these rights
must hold against their fellow-men and must mean that somebody else is to spend his energy to sustain the existence of the
persons so born. What then becomes of the natural rights of the
one whose energies are to be diverted from his own interests? If
it be said that we should all help each other, that means simply
that the race as a whole should advance and expand as much and

as fast as it can in its career on earth; and the experience on which we are now acting has shown that we shall do this best under liberty and under the organization which we are now developing, by leaving each to exert his energies for his own success. The notion of natural rights is destitute of sense, but it is captivating, and it is the more available on account of its vagueness. It lends itself to the most vicious kind of social dogmatism, for if a man has natural rights, then the reasoning is clear up to the finished socialistic doctrine that a man has a natural right to whatever he needs, and that the measure of his claims is the wishes which he wants fulfilled. If, then, he has a need, who is bound to satisfy it for him? Who holds the obligation correspondingly to his right? It must be the one who possesses what will satisfy that need, or else the state which can take the possession from those who have earned and saved it, and give it to him who needs it and who, by the hypothesis, has not earned and saved it.

It is with the next step, however, that we come to the complete and ruinous absurdity of this view. If a man may demand from those who have a share of what he needs and has not, may he demand the same also for his wife and for his children, and for how many children? The industrious and prudent man who takes the course of labor and self-denial to secure capital, finds that he must defer marriage, both in order to save and to devote his life to the education of fewer children. The man who can claim a share in another's product has no such restraint. The consequence would be that the industrious and prudent would labor and save, without families, to support the idle and improvident who would increase and multiply, until universal destitution forced a return to the principles of liberty and property; and the man who started with the notion that the world owed him a living would once more find, as he does now, that the world pays him its debt in the state prison.

The most specious application of the dogma of rights is to labor. It is said that every man has a right to work. The world is full of work to be done. Those who are willing to work find that they have three days' work to do in every day that comes. Work is the necessity to which we are born. It is not a right, but an irksome necessity, and men escape it whenever they can get the fruits of labor without it. What they want is the fruits, or wages, not work. But wages are capital which some one has earned and saved. If he and the workman can agree on the terms on which he will part with his capital, there is no more to be said. If not, then the right must be set up in a new form. It is now not a right to work, nor even a right to wages, but a right to a certain rate of wages, and we have simply returned to the old doctrine of spoliation again. It is immaterial whether the demand for wages be addressed to an individual capitalist or to a civil body, for the latter can give no wages which it does not collect by taxes out of the capital of those who have labored and saved.

Another application is in the attempt to fix the hours of labor *per diem* by law. If a man is forbidden to labor over eight hours per day (and the law has no sense or utility for the purposes of those who want it until it takes this form), he is forbidden to exercise so much industry as he may be willing to expend in order to accumulate capital for the improvement of his circumstances.

A century ago there were very few wealthy men except owners of land. The extension of commerce, manufactures, and mining, the introduction of the factory system and machinery, the opening of new countries, and the great discoveries and inventions have created a new middle class, based on wealth, and developed out of the peasants, artisans, unskilled laborers, and small shop-keepers of a century ago. The consequence has been that the chance of acquiring capital and all which depends on capital has opened before classes which formerly passed their lives in a dull round of ignorance and drudgery. This chance has brought with it the same alternative which accompanies every other opportunity offered to mortals. Those who were wise and able to profit by the chance succeeded grandly; those who were negligent or unable to profit by it suffered proportionately. The result has been wide inequalities of wealth within the industrial classes. The net result, however, for all, has been the cheapening of luxuries and a vast extension of physical enjoyment. The appetite for enjoyment has been awakened and nourished in classes which formerly never missed what they never thought of, and it has produced eagerness for material good, discontent, and impatient ambition. This is the reverse side of that eager uprising of the industrial classes which is such a great force in modern life. The chance is opened to advance, by industry, prudence, economy, and emigration, to the possession of capital; but the way is long and tedious. The impatience for enjoyment and the thirst for luxury which we have mentioned are the greatest foes to the accumulation of capital; and there is a still darker side to the picture when we come to notice that those who yield to the impatience to enjoy, but who see others outstrip them, are led to malice and envy. Mobs arise which manifest the most savage and senseless disposition to burn and destroy what they cannot enjoy. We have already had evidence, in more than one country, that such a wild disposition exists and needs only opportunity to burst into activity.

The origin of socialism, which is the extreme development of the sentimental philosophy, lies in the undisputed facts which I described at the outset. The socialist regards this misery as the fault of society. He thinks that we can organize society as we like and that an organization can be devised in which poverty and misery shall disappear. He goes further even than this. He assumes that men have artificially organized society as it now exists. Hence if anything is disagreeable or hard in the present state of society it follows, on that view, that the task of organizing society has been imperfectly and badly performed, and that it needs to be done over again. These are the assumptions with which the socialist starts, and many socialists seem also to believe that if they can destroy belief in an Almighty God who is supposed to have made the world such as it is, they will then have overthrown the belief that there is a fixed order in human nature and human life which man can scarcely alter at all, and, if at all, only infinitesimally.

The truth is that the social order is fixed by laws of nature precisely analogous to those of the physical order. The most that man can do is by ignorance and self-conceit to mar the operation of social laws. The evils of society are to a great extent the result of the dogmatism and self-interest of statesmen, philosophers, and ecclesiastics who in past time have done just what the socialists now want to do. Instead of studying the natural laws of the social order, they assumed that they could organize society as they chose, they made up their minds what kind of a society they wanted to make, and they planned their little measures for the ends they had resolved upon. It will take centuries of scientific study of the facts of nature to eliminate from human society the mischievous institutions and traditions which the said statesmen, philosophers, and ecclesiastics have introduced into it. Let us not, however, even then delude ourselves with any impossible hopes. The hardships of life would not be eliminated if the laws of nature acted directly and without interference. The task of right living forever changes its form, but let us not imagine that that task will ever reach a final solution or that any race of men on this earth can ever be emancipated from the necessity of industry, prudence, continence, and temperance if they are to pass their lives prosperously. If you believe the contrary you must suppose that some men can come to exist who shall know nothing of old age, disease, and death.

The socialist enterprise of reorganizing society in order to change what is harsh and sad in it at present is therefore as impossible, from the outset, as a plan for changing the physical order. I read the other day a story in which a man dreamt that somebody had invented an application of electricity for eradicating certain facts from the memory. Just think of it! What an emancipation to the human race, if a man could so emancipate himself from all those incidents in his past life which he regrets! Let there no longer be such a thing as remorse or vain regret! It would be half as good as finding a fountain of eternal youth. Or invent us a world in which two and two could make five. Two two-dollar notes could then pay five dollars of debts. They say that political economy is a dismal science and that its doctrines are dark and cruel. I think the hardest fact in human life is that two and two cannot make five; but in sociology while people will agree that two and two cannot make five, yet they think that it might somehow be possible by adjusting two and two to one another in some way or other to make two and two equal to four and one-tenth.

I have shown how men emerge from barbarism only by the use of capital and why it is that, as soon as they begin to use capital, if there is liberty, there will be inequality. The socialist looking at these facts says that it is capital which produces the inequality. It is the inequality of men in what they get out of life which shocks the socialist. He finds enough to criticize in the products of past dogmatism and bad statesmanship to which I have alluded, and the program of reforms to be accomplished and abuses to be rectified which the socialists have set up have often been admirable. It is their analysis of the situation which is at fault. Their diagnosis of the social disease is founded on sectarian assumptions, not on the scientific study of the structure and functions of the social body. In attacking capital they are simply attacking the foundations of civilization, and every socialistic scheme which has ever been proposed, so far as it has lessened the motives to saving or the security of capital, is anti-social and anti-civilizing.

Rousseau, who is the great father of the modern socialism, laid accusation for the inequalities existing amongst men upon wheat and iron. What he meant was that wheat is a symbol of agriculture, and when men took to agriculture and wheat diet they broke up their old tribal relations, which were partly communistic, and developed individualism and private property. At the same time agriculture called for tools and machines, of which iron is a symbol; but these tools and machines are capital. Agriculture, individualism, tools, capital were, according to Rousseau's ideas, the causes of inequality. He was, in a certain way, correct, as we have already seen by our own analysis of the facts of the social order. When human society reached the agricultural stage machinery became necessary. Capital was far more important than on the hunting or pastoral stage, and the inequalities of men were developed with great rapidity, so that we have a Humboldt, a Newton, or a Shakespeare at one end of the scale and a Digger Indian at the other. The Humboldt or Newton is one of the highest products produced by the constant selection and advance of the best part of the human race, *viz.*, those who have seized every chance of advancing; and the Digger Indian is a specimen of that part of the race which withdrew from the competition clear back at the beginning and has consequently never made any advance beyond the first superiority of man to beasts. Rousseau, following the logic of his own explanation of the facts, offered distinctly as the cure for inequality a return to the hunting stage of life as practiced by the American Indians. In this he was plainly and distinctly right. If you want equality you must not look forward for it on the path of advancing civilization. You may go back to the mode of life of the American Indian, and, although you will not then reach equality, you will escape those glaring inequalities of wealth and poverty by coming down to a comparative equality, that is, to a status in which all are equally miserable. Even this, however, you cannot do without submitting to other conditions which are far more appalling than any sad facts in the existing order of society. The population of Massachusetts is about two hundred to the square mile; on the hunting stage Massachusetts could not probably support, at the utmost, five to the square mile; hence to get back to the hunting stage would cost the reduction of the population to two and a half where there are now one hundred. In Rousseau's day people did not even know that this question of the power of land to support population was to be taken into account.

Socialists find it necessary to alter the definition of capital in order to maintain their attacks upon it. Karl Marx, for instance, regards capital as an accumulation of the differences which a merchant makes between his buying price and his selling price. It is, according to him, an accumulation of the differences which the employer gains between what he pays to the employees for making the thing and what he obtains for it from the consumer. In this view of the matter the capitalist employer is a pure parasite, who has fastened on the wage-receiving employee without need or reason and is levying toll on industry. All socialistic writers follow, in different degrees, this conception of capital. If it is true, why do not I levy on some workers somewhere and steal this difference in the product of their labor? Is it because I am more honest or magnanimous than those who are capitalist-employers? I should not trust myself to resist the chance if I had it. Or again, let us ask why, if this conception of the origin of capital is correct, the workmen submit to a pure and un-necessary imposition. If this notion were true, co-operation in production would not need any effort to bring it about; it would take an army to keep it down. The reason why it is not possible for the first comer to start out as an employer of labor is that capital is a prerequisite to all industry. So soon as men pass beyond the stage of life in which they live, like beasts, on the spontaneous fruits of the earth, capital must precede every productive enterprise. It would lead me too far away from my present subject to elaborate this statement as it deserves and perhaps as it needs, but I may say that there is no sound political economy and especially no correct conception of wages which is not based on a complete recognition of the character of capital as necessarily going before every industrial operation. The reason why co-operation in production is exceedingly difficult, and indeed is not possible except in the highest and rarest conditions of education and culture amongst artisans, is that workmen cannot undertake an enterprise without capital, and that capital always means the fruits of prudence and self-denial already accomplished. The capitalist's profits, therefore, are only the reward for the contribution he has made to a joint enterprise which could not go on without him, and his share is as legitimate as that of the hand-worker.

The socialist assails particularly the institution of bequest or hereditary property, by which some men come into life with special protection and advantage. The right of bequest rests on no other grounds than those of expediency. The love of children is the strongest motive to frugality and to the accumulation of capital. The state guarantees the power of bequest only because it thereby encourages the accumulation of capital on which the welfare of society depends. It is true enough that inherited capital often proves a curse. Wealth is like health, physical strength, education, or anything else which enhances the power of the individual; it is only a chance; its moral character depends entirely upon the use which is made of it. Any force which, when well used, is capable of elevating a man, will, if abused, debase him in the same proportion. This is true of education, which is often and incorrectly vaunted as a positive

and purely beneficent instrumentality. An education ill used
makes a man only a more mischievous scoundrel, just as an
education well used makes him a more efficient, good citizen and
producer. So it is with wealth; it is a means to all the higher
developments of intellectual and moral culture. A man of inherited wealth can gain in youth all the advantages which are
essential to high culture, and which a man who must first earn
the capital cannot attain until he is almost past the time of life
for profiting by them. If one should believe the newspapers,
one would be driven to a philosophy something like this: it is
extremely praiseworthy for a man born in poverty to accumulate
a fortune; the reason why he wants to secure a fortune is that
he wants to secure the position of his children and start them
with better advantages than he enjoyed himself; this is a noble
desire on his part, but he really ought to doubt and hesitate
about so doing because the chances are that he would do far
better for his children to leave them poor. The children who
inherit his wealth are put under suspicion by it; it creates a
presumption against them in all the activities of citizenship.

Now it is no doubt true that the struggle to win a fortune
gives strength of character and a practical judgment and efficiency which a man who inherits wealth rarely gets, but hereditary wealth transmitted from generation to generation is the
strongest instrument by which we keep up a steadily advancing
civilization. In the absence of laws of entail and perpetuity it is
inevitable that capital should speedily slip from the hold of the
man who is not fit to possess it, back into the great stream of
capital, and so find its way into the hands of those who can use
it for the benefit of society.

The love of children is an instinct which, as I have said before, grows stronger with advancing civilization. All attacks on
capital have, up to this time, been shipwrecked on this instinct.
Consequently the most rigorous and logical socialists have always been led sooner or later to attack the family. For, if bequest
should be abolished, parents would give their property to their
children in their own life-time; and so it becomes a logical necessity to substitute some sort of communistic or socialistic life for
family life, and to educate children in masses without the tie

of parentage. Every socialistic theory which has been pursued energetically has led out to this consequence. I will not follow up this topic, but it is plain to see that the only equality which could be reached on this course would be that men should be all equal to each other when they were all equal to swine.

Socialists are filled with the enthusiasm of equality. Every scheme of theirs for securing equality has destroyed liberty. The student of political philosophy has the antagonism of equality and liberty constantly forced upon him. Equality of possession or of rights and equality before the law are diametrically opposed to each other. The object of equality before the law is to make the state entirely neutral. The state, under that theory, takes no cognizance of persons. It surrounds all, without distinctions, with the same conditions and guarantees. If it educates one, it educates all—black, white, red, or yellow; Jew or Gentile; native or alien. If it taxes one, it taxes all, by the same system and under the same conditions. If it exempts one from police regulations in home, church, and occupation, it exempts all. From this statement it is at once evident that pure equality before the law is impossible. Some occupations must be subjected to police regulation. Not all can be made subject to militia duty even for the same limited period. The exceptions and special cases furnish the chance for abuse. Equality before the law, however, is one of the cardinal principles of civil liberty, because it leaves each man to run the race of life for himself as best he can. The state stands neutral but benevolent. It does not undertake to aid some and handicap others at the outset in order to offset hereditary advantages and disadvantages, or to make them start equally. Such a notion would belong to the false and spurious theory of equality which is socialistic. If the state should attempt this it would make itself the servant of envy. I am entitled to make the most I can of myself without hindrance from anybody, but I am not entitled to any guarantee that I shall make as much of myself as somebody else makes of himself.

The modern thirst for equality of rights is explained by its historical origin. The mediæval notion of rights was that rights were special privileges, exemptions, franchises, and powers given to individuals by the king; hence each man had just so many as he and his ancestors had been able to buy or beg by force or favor, and if a man had obtained no grants he had no rights. Hence no two persons were equal in rights and the mass of the population had none. The theory of natural rights and of equal rights was a revolt against the mediæval theory. It was asserted that men did not have to wait for a king to grant them rights; they have them by nature, or in the nature of things, because they are men and members of civil society. If rights come from nature, it is inferred that they fall like air and light on all equally. It was an immense step in advance for the human race when this new doctrine was promulgated. Its own limitations and errors need not now be pointed out. Its significance is plain, and its limits are to some extent defined when we note its historical origin.

I have already shown that where these guarantees exist and where there is liberty, the results cannot be equal, but with all liberty there must go responsibility. If I take my own way I must take my own consequences; if it proves that I have made a mistake, I cannot be allowed to throw the consequences on my neighbor. If my neighbor is a free man and resents interference from me he must not call on me to bear the consequences of his mistakes. Hence it is plain that liberty, equality before the law, responsibility, individualism, monogamy, and private propetry all hold together as consistent parts of the same structure of society, and that an assault on one part must sooner or later involve an assault on all the others.

To all this must be added the political element in socialism. The acquisition of some capital—the amount is of very subordinate importance—is the first and simplest proof that an individual possesses the industrial and civil virtues which make a good citizen and a useful member of society. Political power, a century ago, was associated more or less, even in the United States, with the possession of land. It has been gradually extended until the suffrage is to all intents and purposes universal in North and South America, in Australia, and in all Europe except Russia and Turkey. On this system political control belongs to the numerical majority, limited only by institutions. It may be doubted, if the terms are taken strictly and correctly, whether the non-capitalists outnumber the capitalists in any civilized country, but in many cities where capital is most collected they certainly do. The powers of government have been abused for ages by the classes who possessed them to enable kings, courtiers, nobles, politicians, demagogues, and their friends to live in exemption from labor and self-denial, that is, from the universal lot of man. It is only a continuation of the same abuse if the new possessors of power attempt to employ it to secure for themselves the selfish advantages which all possessors of power have taken. Such a course would, however, overthrow all that we think has been won in the way of making government an organ of justice, peace, order, and security, without respect of persons; and if those gains are not to be lost they will have to be defended, before this century closes, against popular majorities, especially in cities, just as they had to be won in a struggle with kings and nobles in the centuries past.

The newest socialism is, in its method, political. The essential feature of its latest phases is the attempt to use the power of the state to realize its plans and to secure its objects. These objects are to do away with poverty and misery, and there are no socialistic schemes yet proposed, of any sort, which do not, upon analysis, turn out to be projects for curing poverty and misery by making those who have share with those who have not. Whether they are paper-money schemes, tariff schemes, subsidy schemes, internal improvement schemes, or usury laws, they all have this in common with the most vulgar of the communistic projects, and the errors of this sort in the past which have been committed in the interest of the capitalist class now furnish precedents, illustration, and encouragement for the new category of demands. The latest socialism divides into two phases: one which aims at centralization and despotism—believing that political form more available for its purposes; the other, the anarchical, which prefers to split up the state into townships, or "communes," to the same end. The latter furnishes the true etymology and meaning of "communism" in its present use, but all socialism, in its second stage, merges into a division of property according to the old sense of communism.

It is impossible to notice socialism as it presents itself at the present moment without pointing out the immense mischief which has been done by sentimental economists and social philosophers who have thought it their professional duty, not to investigate and teach the truth, but to dabble in philanthropy. It is in Germany that this development has been most marked, and as a consequence of it the judgment and sense of the whole people in regard to political and social questions have been corrupted. It is remarkable that the country whose learned men have wrought so much for every other science, especially by virtue of their scientific method and rigorous critical processes, should have furnished a body of social philosophers without method, discipline, or severity of scholarship, who have led the nation in pursuit of whims and dreams and impossible desires. Amongst us there has been less of it, for our people still possess enough sterling sense to reject sentimental rubbish in its grosser forms, but we have had and still have abundance of the more subtle forms of socialistic doctrine, and these open the way to the others. We may already see the two developments forming a congenial alliance. We have also our writers and teachers who seem to think that "the weak" and "the poor" are terms of exact definition; that government exists, in some especial sense, for the sake of the classes so designated; and that the same classes (whoever they are) have some especial claim on the interest and attention of the economist and social philosopher. It may be believed that, in the opinion of these persons, the training of men is the only branch of human effort in which the labor and care should be spent, not on the best specimens but on the poorest.

It is a matter of course that a reactionary party should arise to declare that universal suffrage, popular education, machinery, free trade, and all the other innovations of the last hundred years are all a mistake. If any one ever believed that these innovations were so many clear strides towards the millennium, that they involve no evils or abuses of their own, that they tend to emancipate mankind from the need for prudence, caution, forethought, vigilance—in short, from the eternal struggle against evil—it is not strange that he should be disappointed. If any one ever believed that some "form of government" could be found which would run itself and turn out the pure results of abstract peace, justice, and righteousness without any trouble to anybody, he may well be dissatisfied. To talk of turning back, however, is only to enhance still further the confusion and danger of our position. The world cannot go back. Its destiny is to go forward and to meet the new problems which are continually arising. Under our so-called progress evil only alters its forms, and we must esteem it a grand advance if we can believe that, on the whole, and over a wide view of human affairs, good has gained a hair's breadth over evil in a century. Popular institutions have their own abuses and dangers just as much as monarchical or aristocratic institutions. We are only just finding out what they are. All the institutions which we have inherited were invented to guard liberty against the encroachments of a powerful monarch or aristocracy, when these classes possessed land and the possession of land was the greatest social power. Institutions must now be devised to guard civil liberty against popular majorities, and this necessity arises first in regard to the protection of property, the first and greatest function of government and element in civil liberty. There is no escape from any dangers involved in this or any other social struggle save in going forward and working out the development. It will cost a struggle and will demand the highest wisdom of this and the next generation. It is very probable that some nations—those, namely, which come up to this problem with the least preparation, with the least intelligent comprehension of the problem, and under the most inefficient leadership—will suffer a severe check in their development and prosperity; it is very probable that in some nations the development may lead through revolution and bloodshed; it is very probable that in some nations the consequence may be a reaction towards arbitrary power. In every view we take of it, it is clear that the general abolition of slavery has only cleared the way for a new social problem of far wider scope and far greater difficulty. It seems to me, in fact, that this must always be the case. The conquest of one difficulty will only open the way to another; the solution of one problem will only bring man face to face with another. Man wins by the fight, not by the victory, and therefore the possibilities of growth are unlimited, for the fight has no end.

The progress which men have made in developing the possibilities of human existence has never been made by jumps and strides. It has never resulted from the schemes of philosophers and reformers. It has never been guided through a set program by the wisdom of any sages, statesmen, or philanthropists. The progress which has been made has been won in minute stages by men who had a definite task before them, and who have dealt with it in detail, as it presented itself, without referring to general principles, or attempting to bring it into logical relations to an *a priori* system. In most cases the agents are unknown and cannot be found. New and better arrangements have grown up imperceptibly by the natural effort of all to make the best of actual circumstances. In this way, no doubt, the new problems arising in our modern society must be solved or must solve themselves. The chief safeguard and hope of such a development is in the sound instincts and strong sense of the people, which, although it may not reason closely, can reject instinctively. If there are laws—and there certainly are such—which permit the acquisition of property without industry, by cunning, force, gambling, swindling, favoritism, or corruption, such laws transfer property from those who have earned it to those who have not. Such laws contain the radical vice of socialism. They demand correction and offer an open field for reform because reform would lie in the direction of greater purity and security of the right of property. Whatever assails that right, or goes in the direction of making it still more uncertain whether the industrious man can dispose of the fruits of his industry for his own interests exclusively, tends directly towards violence, bloodshed, poverty, and misery. If any large section of modern society should rise against the rest for the purpose of attempting any such spoliation, either by violence or through the forms of law, it would destroy civilization as it was destroyed by the irruption of the barbarians into the Roman Empire.

The sound student of sociology can hold out to mankind, as individuals or as a race, only one hope of better and happier living. That hope lies in an enhancement of the industrial virtues and of the moral forces which thence arise. Industry, self-denial, and temperance are the laws of prosperity for men and states; without them advance in the arts and in wealth means only corruption and decay through luxury and vice. With them progress in the arts and increasing wealth are the prime conditions of an advancing civilization which is sound enough to endure. The power of the human race to-day over the conditions of prosperous and happy living are sufficient to banish poverty and misery if it were not for folly and vice. The earth does not begin to be populated up to its power to support population on the present stage of the arts; if the United States were as densely populated as the British Islands, we should have 1,000,000,000 people here. If, therefore, men were willing to set to work with energy and courage to subdue the outlying parts of the earth, all might live in plenty and prosperity. But if they insist on remaining in the slums of great cities or on the borders of an old society, and on a comparatively exhausted soil, there is no device of economist or statesman which can prevent them from falling victims to poverty and misery or from succumbing in the competition of life to those who have greater command of capital. The socialist or philanthropist who nourishes them in their situation and saves them from the distress of it is only cultivating the distress which he pretends to cure.

VI

State Interference

I desire, in this paper, to give an explanation and justification of extreme prejudice against State interference, and I wish to begin with a statement from history of the effect upon the individual of various forms of the State.

It appears, from the best evidence we possess, according to the most reasonable interpretation which has been given to it, that the internal organization of society owes its cohesion and intensity to the necessity of meeting pressure from without. A band of persons, bound by ties of neighborhood or kin, clung together in order to maintain their common interests against a similar band of their neighbors. The social bond and the common interest were at war with individual interests. They exerted coercive power to crush individualism, to produce uniformity, to proscribe dissent, to make private judgment a social offense, and to exercise drill and discipline.

In the Roman State the internal discipline gave victory in contests with neighbors. Each member of the Roman community was carried up by the success of the body of which he was a member to the position of a world-conqueror. Then the Roman community split up into factions to quarrel for the spoils of the world, until the only escape from chronic civil war and anarchy was a one-man power, which, however, proved only a mode of disintegration and decay, not a cure for it. It has often been remarked with astonishment how lightly men and women of rank at Rome in the first century of our era held their lives. They seem to have been ready to open their veins at a moment's notice, and to quit life upon trivial occasion. If we can realize what life must have been in such a State we can, perhaps, understand this. The Emperor was the State. He was a mortal who had been freed from all care for the rights of others, and his own passions had all been set free. Any man or woman in the civilized world was at the mercy of his caprices. Anyone who was great enough to attract his attention, especially by the possession of anything which mortals covet, held his life at the utmost peril. Since the Empire was the world, there was no escape save to get out of the world. Many seemed to hold escape cheap at that price.

At first under the Empire the obscure people were safe. They probably had little to complain of, and found the Empire gay and beneficent; but it gradually and steadily absorbed every rank and interest into its pitiless organization. At last industry and commerce as well as all civil and social duties took the form of State functions. The ideal which some of our modern social philosophers are preaching was realized. The State was an ethical person, in the strictest sense of the word, when it was one man and when every duty and interest of life was construed towards him. All relations were regulated according to the ethics of the time, which is, of course, all that ethical regulation ever can amount to. Every duty of life took the form and name of an "obsequium"; that is, of a function in the State organism.

Now the most important relation of the citizen to the State is that of a soldier, and the next is that of a taxpayer, and when the former loses importance the latter becomes the chief. Accordingly the obsequia of the citizens in the later centuries were regulated in such a way that the citizen might contribute most to the fiscus. He was not only made part of a machine, but it was a tax-paying machine, and all his hopes, rights, interests, and human capabilities were merged in this purpose of his existence. Slavery, as we ordinarily understand the term, died out, but it gave way to a servitude of each to all, when each was locked tight in an immense and artificial organization of society.

Such must ever be the effect of merging industry in the State. Every attempt of the Roman handicraftsmen to better themselves was a breach of the peace; disobedience was rebellion; resistance was treason; running away was desertion.

Here, then, we have a long history, in which the State power first served the national interest in contest with outside powers, and then itself became a burden and drew all the life out of the subject population.

In the Middle Ages a society which had been resolved into its simple elements had to re-form. The feudal form was imposed upon it by the conditions and elements of the case. It was as impossible for a man to stand alone as it had been on the hunting or pastoral stage of life or on the lower organizations of civilization. There was once more necessity to yield personal liberty in order to get protection against plunder from others, and in order to obtain this protection it was necessary to get into a group and to conform to its organization. Here again the same difficulty soon presented itself. Protection against outside aggression was won, but the protecting power itself became a plunderer.

This oppression brought about guild and other organizations for mutual defense. Sometimes these organizations themselves won civil power; sometimes they were under some political sovereign, but possessed its sanction. The system which grew up was one of complete regulation and control. The guilds were regulated in every function and right. The masters, journeymen, and apprentices were regulated in their relations and in all their rights and duties. The work of supplying a certain community with any of the necessaries of life was regarded as a privilege and was monopolized by a certain number. The mediæval system, however, did not allow this monopoly to be exploited at the expense of consumers, according to the good will of the holders of it. The sovereign interfered constantly, and at all points, wherever its intervention was asked for. It fixed prices, but it also fixed wages, regulated kinds and prices of raw materials, prescribed the relation of one trade to another, forbade touting, advertising, rivalry; regulated buying and selling by merchants; protected consumers by inspection; limited importations, but might force production and force sales.

Here was plainly a complete system, which had a rational motive and a logical method. The object was to keep all the organs of society in their accepted relations to each other and to preserve all in activity in the measure of the social needs. The plan failed entirely. It was an impossible undertaking, even on the narrow arena of a mediæval city. The ordinances of an authority which stood ready to interfere at any time and in any way were necessarily inconsistent and contradictory. Its effect upon those who could not get into the system—that is, upon the vagabondage of the period—has never, so far as I know, been studied carefully, although that is the place to look for its most distinct social effect. The most interesting fact about it, however, is that the privilege of one age became the bondage of the next and that the organization which had grown up for the mutual defense of the artisans lost its original purpose and became a barrier to the rise of the artisan class. The organization was a fetter on individual enterprise and success.

The fact should not be overlooked here that, if we are to have the mediæval system of regulation revived, we want it altogether. That system was not, in intention, unjust. According to its light it aimed at the welfare of all. It was not its motive to give privileges, but a system of partial interference is sure to be a system of favoritism and injustice. It is a system of charters to some to plunder others. A mediæval sovereign would never interfere with railroads on behalf of shippers and stop there. He would fix the interest on bonds and other fixed charges. He would, upon appeal, regulate the wages of employees. He would fix the price of coal and other supplies. He would never admit that he was the guardian of one interest more than another, and he would interfere over and over again as often as stockholders, bondholders, employees, shippers, etc., could persuade him that they had a grievance. He would do mischief over and over again, but he would not do intentional injustice.

After the mediæval system broke up and the great modern States formed, the royal power became the representative and champion of national interests in modern Europe, and it established itself in approximately absolute power by the fact that the interest of the nations to maintain themselves in the rivalry of States seemed the paramount interest. Within a few months we have seen modern Germany discard every other interest in order to respond to the supposed necessity of military defense. Not very long ago, in our Civil War, we refused to take account of anything else until the military task was accomplished.

In all these cases the fact appears that the interest of the individual and the social interest have been at war with each other, while, again, the interests of the individual in and through the society of which he is a member are inseparable from those of the society. Such are the two aspects of the relation of the unit and the whole which go to make the life of the race. The individual has an interest to develop all the personal elements there are in him. He wants to live himself out. He does not want to be planed down to a type or pattern. It is the interest of society that all the original powers it contains should be brought out to their full value. But the social movement is coercive and uniformitarian. Organization and discipline are essential to effective common action, and they crush out individual enterprise and personal variety. There is only one kind of cooperation which escapes this evil, and that is cooperation which is voluntary and automatic, under common impulses and natural laws. State control, however, is always necessary for national action in the family of nations and to prevent plunder by others, and men have never yet succeeded in getting it without falling under the necessity of submitting to plunder at home from those on whom they rely for defense abroad.

Now, at the height of our civilization and with the best light that we can bring to bear on our social relations, the problem is: Can we get from the State security for individuals to pursue happiness in and under it, and yet not have the State itself become a new burden and hindrance only a little better than the evil which it wards off?

It is only in the most recent times, and in such measure as the exigencies of external defense have been diminished by the partial abandonment of motives of plunder and conquest, that there has been a chance for individualism to grow. In the latest times the struggle for a relaxation of political bonds on behalf of individual liberty has taken the form of breaking the royal power and forcing the king to take his hands off. Liberty has hardly yet come to be popularly understood as anything else but republicanism or anti-royalty.

The United States, starting on a new continent, with full chance to select the old-world traditions which they would adopt, have become the representatives and champions in modern times of all the principles of individualism and personal liberty. We have had no neighbors to fear. We have had no necessity for stringent State discipline. Each one of us has been able to pursue happiness in his own way, unhindered by the demands of a State which would have worn out our energies by expenditure simply in order to maintain the State. The State has existed of itself. The one great exception, the Civil War, only illustrates the point more completely *per contra*. The old Jeffersonian party rose to power and held it, because it conformed to the genius of the country and bore along the true destinies of a nation situated as this one was. It is the glory of the United States, and its calling in history, that it shows what the power of personal liberty is—what self-reliance, energy, enterprise, hard sense men can develop when they have room and liberty and when they are emancipated from the burden of traditions and faiths which are nothing but the accumulated follies and blunders of a hundred generations of "statesmen."

It is, therefore, the highest product of political institutions so far that they have come to a point where, under favorable circumstances, individualism is, under their protection, to some extent possible. If political institutions can give security for the pursuit of happiness by each individual, according to his own notion of it, in his own way, and by his own means, they have reached their perfection. This fact, however, has two aspects. If no man can be held to serve another man's happiness, it follows that no man can call on another to serve his happiness. The different views of individualism depend on which of these aspects is under observation. What seems to be desired now is a combination of liberty for all with an obligation of each to all. That is one of the forms in which we are seeking a social philosopher's stone.

The reflex influence which American institutions have had on

European institutions is well known. We have had to take as well as give. When the United States put upon their necks the yoke of a navigation and colonial system which they had just revolted against, they showed how little possible it is, after all, for men to rise above the current notions of their time, even when geographical and economic circumstances favor their emancipation. We have been borrowing old-world fashions and traditions all through our history, instead of standing firmly by the political and social philosophy of which we are the standard-bearers.

So long as a nation has not lost faith in itself it is possible for it to remodel its institutions to any extent. If it gives way to sentimentalism, or sensibility, or political mysticism, or adopts an affectation of radicalism, or any other *ism,* or molds its institutions so as to round out to a more complete fulfillment somebody's theory of the universe, it may fall into an era of revolution and political insecurity which will break off the continuity of its national life and make orderly and secure progress impossible. Now that the royal power is limited, and that the old military and police States are in the way of transition to jural States, we are promised a new advance to democracy. What is the disposition of the new State as regards the scope of its power? It unquestionably manifests a disposition to keep and use the whole arsenal of its predecessors. The great engine of political abuse has always been political mysticism. Formerly we were told of the divine origin of the State and the divine authority of rulers. The mystical contents of "sovereignty" have always provided an inexhaustible source of dogma and inference for any extension of State power. The new democracy, having inherited the power so long used against it, now shows every disposition to use that power as ruthlessly as any other governing organ ever has used it.

We are told that the State is an ethical person. This is the latest form of political mysticism. Now, it is true that the State is an ethical person in just the same sense as a business firm, a joint stock corporation, or a debating society. It is not a physical person, but it may be a metaphysical or legal person, and as such it has an entity and is an independent subject of rights and duties. Like the other ethical persons, however, the State is just good for what it can do to serve the interests of man, and no more. Such is far from being the meaning and utility of the dogma that the State is an ethical person. The dogma is needed as a source from which can be spun out again contents of phrases and deductions previously stowed away in it. It is only the most modern form of dogmatism devised to sacrifice the man to the institution which is not good for anything except so far as it can serve the man.

One of the newest names for the coming power is the "omnicracy." Mankind has been trying for some thousands of years to find the right -ocracy. None of those which have yet been tried have proved satisfactory. We want a new name on which to pin new hopes, for mankind "never is, but always to be blessed." Omnicracy has this much sense in it, that no one of the great dogmas of the modern political creed is true if it is affirmed of anything less than the whole population, man, woman, child, and baby. When the propositions are enunciated in this sense they are philosophically grand and true. For instance, all the propositions about the "people" are grand and true if we mean by the people every soul in the community, with all the interests and powers which give them an aggregate will and power, with capacity to suffer or to work; but then, also, the propositions remain grand abstractions beyond the realm of practical utility. On the other hand, those propositions cannot be made practically available unless they are affirmed of some limited section of the population, for instance, a majority of the males over twenty-one; but then they are no longer true in philosophy or in fact.

Consequently, when the old-fashioned theories of State interference are applied to the new democratic State, they turn out to be simply a device for setting separate interests in a struggle against each other inside the society. It is plain on the face of all the great questions which are offered to us as political questions to-day, that they are simply struggles of interests for larger shares of the product of industry. One mode of dealing with this distribution would be to leave it to free contract under the play of natural laws. If we do not do this, and if the State interferes with the distribution, how can we stop short of the mediæval plan of reiterated and endless interference, with constant diminution of the total product to be divided?

We have seen above what the tyranny was in the decay of the Roman Empire, when each was in servitude to all; but there is one form of that tyranny which may be still worse. That tyranny will be realized when the same system of servitudes is established in a democratic state; when a man's neighbors are his masters; when the "ethical power of public opinion" bears down upon him at all hours and as to all matters; when his place is assigned to him and he is held in it, not by an emperor or his satellites, who cannot be everywhere all the time, but by the other members of the "village community" who can.

So long as the struggle for individual liberty took the form of a demand that the king or the privileged classes should take their hands off, it was popular and was believed to carry with it the cause of justice and civilization. Now that the governmental machine is brought within everyone's reach, the seduction of power is just as masterful over a democratic faction as ever it was over king or barons. No governing organ has yet abstained from any function because it acknowledged itself ignorant or incompetent. The new powers in the State show no disposition to do it. Nevertheless, the activity of the State, under the new democratic system, shows itself every year more at the mercy of clamorous factions, and legislators find themselves constantly under greater pressure to act, not by their deliberate judgment of what is expedient, but in such a way as to quell clamor, although against their judgment of public interests. It is rapidly becoming the chief art of the legislator to devise measures which shall sound as if they satisfied clamor while they only cheat it.

There are two things which are often treated as if they were identical, which are as far apart as any two things in the field of political philosophy can be: (1) That everyone should be left to do as he likes, so far as possible, without any other social restraints than such as are unavoidable for the peace and order of society. (2) That "the people" should be allowed to carry out their will without any restraint from constitutional institutions. The former means that each should have his own way with his own interests; the latter, that any faction which for the time is uppermost should have its own way with all the rest.

One result of all the new State interference is that the State is being superseded in vast domains of its proper work. While it is reaching out on one side to fields of socialistic enterprise, interfering in the interests of parties in the industrial organism, assuming knowledge of economic laws which nobody possesses, taking ground as to dogmatic notions of justice which are absurd, and acting because it does not know what to do, it is losing its power to give peace, order, and security. The extra-legal power and authority of leaders over voluntary organizations of men throughout a community who are banded together in order to press their interests at the expense of other interests, and who go to the utmost verge of the criminal law, if they do not claim immunity from it, while obeying an authority which acts in secret and without responsibility, is a phenomenon which shows the inadequacy of the existing State to guarantee rights and give security. The boycott and the plan of campaign are certainly not industrial instrumentalities, and it is not yet quite certain whether they are violent and criminal instrumentalities, by which some men coerce other men in matters of material interests. If we turn our minds to the victims of these devices, we see that they do not find in the modern State that security for their interests under the competition of life which it is the first and unquestioned duty of the State to provide. The boycotted man is deprived of the peaceful enjoyment of rights which the laws and institutions of his country allow him, and he has no redress. The State has forbidden all private war on the ground that it will give a remedy for wrongs, and that private redress would disturb the peaceful prosecution of their own interests by other members of the community who are not parties to the quarrel; but we have seen an industrial war paralyze a whole section for weeks, and it was treated almost as a right of the parties that they might fight it out, no matter at what cost to bystanders. We have seen representative bodies of various voluntary associations meet and organize by the side of the regular constitutional organs of the State, in order to deliberate on proposed measures and to transmit to the authorized representatives of the people their approval or disapproval of the propositions, and it scarcely caused a comment. The plutocracy invented the lobby, but the democracy here also seems determined to better the instruction. There are various opinions as to what the revolution is which is upon us, and as to what it is which is about to perish. I do not see anything else which is in as great peril as representative institutions or the constitutional State.

I therefore maintain that it is at the present time a matter of patriotism and civic duty to resist the extension of State interference. It is one of the proudest results of political growth that we have reached the point where individualism is possible. Nothing could better show the merit and value of the institutions which we have inherited than the fact that we can afford to play with all these socialistic and semi-socialistic absurdities. They have no great importance until the question arises: Will a generation which can be led away into this sort of frivolity be able to transmit intact institutions which were made only by men of sterling thought and power, and which can be maintained only by men of the same type? I am familiar with the irritation and impatience with which remonstrances on this matter are received. Those who know just how the world ought to be reconstructed are, of course, angry when they are pushed aside as busybodies. A group of people who assail the legislature with a plan for regulating their neighbor's mode of living are enraged at the "dogma" of non-interference. The publicist who has been struck by some of the superficial roughnesses in the collision of interests which must occur in any time of great industrial activity, and who has therefore determined to waive the objections to State interference, if he can see it brought to bear on his pet reform, will object to absolute principles. For my part, I have never seen that public or private principles were good for anything except when there seemed to be a motive for breaking them. Anyone who has studied a question as to which the solution is yet wanting may despair of the power of free contract to solve it. I have examined a great many cases of proposed interference with free contract, and the only alternative to free contract which I can find is "heads I win, tails you lose" in favor of one party or the other. I am familiar with the criticisms which some writers claim to make upon individualism, but the worst individualism I can find in history is that of the Jacobins, and I believe that it is logically sound that the anti-social vices should be most developed whenever the attempt is made to put socialistic theories in practice. The only question at this point is: Which may we better trust, the play of free social forces or legislative and administrative interference? This question is as pertinent for those who expect to win by interference as for others, for whenever we try to get paternalized we only succeed in getting policed.

VII

The Forgotten Man

I propose in this lecture to discuss one of the most subtle and widespread social fallacies. It consists in the impression made on the mind for the time being by a particular fact, or by the interests of a particular group of persons, to which attention is directed while other facts or the interests of other persons are entirely left out of account. I shall give a number of instances and illustrations of this in a moment, and I cannot expect you to understand what is meant from an abstract statement until these illustrations are before you, but just by way of a general illustration I will put one or two cases.

Whenever a pestilence like yellow fever breaks out in any city, our attention is especially attracted towards it, and our sympathies are excited for the sufferers. If contributions are called for, we readily respond. Yet the number of persons who die prematurely from consumption every year greatly exceeds the deaths from yellow fever or any similar disease when it occurs, and the suffering entailed by consumption is very much greater. The suffering from consumption, however, never constitutes a public question or a subject of social discussion. If an inundation takes place anywhere, constituting a public calamity (and an inundation takes place somewhere in the civilized world nearly every year), public attention is attracted and public appeals are made, but the losses by great inundations must be insignificant compared with the losses by runaway horses, which, taken separately,

scarcely obtain mention in a local newspaper. In hard times insolvent debtors are a large class. They constitute an interest and
are able to attract public attention, so that social philosophers
discuss their troubles and legislatures plan measures of relief.
able to satisfy creditors
Insolvent debtors, however, are an insignificant body compared
with the victims of commonplace misfortune, or accident, who
are isolated, scattered, ungrouped and ungeneralized, and so are
never made the object of discussion or relief. In seasons of ordinary prosperity, persons who become insolvent have to get out
of their troubles as they can. They have no hope of relief from
the legislature. The number of insolvents during a series of years
of general prosperity, and their losses, greatly exceed the number
and losses during a special period of distress.

These illustrations bring out only one side of my subject, and
that only partially. It is when we come to the proposed measures
of relief for the evils which have caught public attention that we
reach the real subject which deserves our attention. As soon as A
observes something which seems to him to be wrong, from which
X is suffering, A talks it over with B, and A and B then propose
to get a law passed to remedy the evil and help X. Their law
always proposes to determine what C shall do for X or, in the
better case, what A, B and C shall do for X. As for A and B, who
get a law to make themselves do for X what they are willing to do
for him, we have nothing to say except that they might better
have done it without any law, but what I want to do is to look
up C. I want to show you what manner of man he is. I call him
the Forgotten Man. Perhaps the appellation is not strictly correct.
He is the man who never is thought of. He is the victim of the
reformer, social speculator and philanthropist, and I hope to
show you before I get through that he deserves your notice both
for his character and for the many burdens which are laid upon
him.

No doubt one great reason for the phenomenon which I bring
to your attention is the passion for reflection and generalization
which marks our period. Since the printing press has come into
such wide use, we have all been encouraged to philosophize about
things in a way which was unknown to our ancestors. They lived
their lives out in positive contact with actual cases as they arose.

They had little of this analysis, introspection, reflection and
speculation which have passed into a habit and almost into a
disease with us. Of all things which tempt to generalization and
to philosophizing, social topics stand foremost. Each one of us
gets some experience of social forces. Each one has some chance
for observation of social phenomena. There is certainly no domain in which generalization is easier. There is nothing about
which people dogmatize more freely. Even men of scientific training in some department in which they would not tolerate dogmatism at all will not hesitate to dogmatize in the most reckless
manner about social topics. The truth is, however, that science,
as yet, has won less control of social phenomena than of any
other class of phenomena. The most complex and difficult subject
which we now have to study is the constitution of human society,
the forces which operate in it, and the laws by which they act,
and we know less about these things than about any others which
demand our attention. In such a state of things, over-hasty generalization is sure to be extremely mischievous. You cannot take
up a magazine or newspaper without being struck by the feverish
interest with which social topics and problems are discussed, and
if you were a student of social science, you would find in almost
all these discussions evidence, not only that the essential preparation for the discussion is wanting, but that the disputants do not
even know that there is any preparation to be gained. Consequently we are bewildered by contradictory dogmatizing. We find
in all these discussions only the application of pet notions and
the clashing of contradictory "views." Remedies are confidently
proposed for which there is no guarantee offered except that the
person who prescribes the remedy says that he is sure it will work.
We hear constantly of "reform," and the reformers turn out to
be people who do not like things as they are and wish that they
could be made nicer. We hear a great many exhortations to make
progress from people who do not know in what direction they
want to go. Consequently social reform is the most barren and
tiresome subject of discussion amongst us, except æsthetics.

I suppose that the first chemists seemed to be very hard-hearted
and unpoetical persons when they scouted the glorious dream of
the alchemists that there must be some process for turning base

metals into gold. I suppose that the men who first said, in plain, cold assertion, there is no fountain of eternal youth, seemed to be the most cruel and cold-hearted adversaries of human happiness. I know that the economists who say that if we could transmute lead into gold, it would certainly do us no good and might do great harm, are still regarded as unworthy of belief. Do not the money articles of the newspapers yet ring with the doctrine that we are getting rich when we give cotton and wheat for gold rather than when we give cotton and wheat for iron?

Let us put down now the cold, hard fact and look at it just as it is. There is no device whatever to be invented for securing happiness without industry, economy, and virtue. We are yet in the empirical stage as regards all our social devices. We have done something in science and art in the domain of production, transportation and exchange. But when you come to the laws of the social order, we know very little about them. Our laws and institutions by which we attempt to regulate our lives under the laws of nature which control society are merely a series of haphazard experiments. We come into collision with the laws and are not intelligent enough to understand wherein we are mistaken and how to correct our errors. We persist in our experiments instead of patiently setting about the study of the laws and facts in order to see where we are wrong. Traditions and formulæ have a dominion over us in legislation and social customs which we seem unable to break or even to modify.

For my present purpose I ask your attention for a few moments to the notion of liberty, because the Forgotten Man would no longer be forgotten where there was true liberty. You will say that you know what liberty is. There is no term of more common or prouder use. None is more current, as if it were quite beyond the need of definition. Even as I write, however, I find in a leading review a new definition of civil liberty. Civil liberty the writer declares to be "the result of the restraint exercised by the sovereign people on the more powerful individuals and classes of the community, preventing them from availing themselves of the excess of their power to the detriment of the other classes." You notice here the use of the words "sovereign people" to designate a class of the population, not the nation as a political

and civil whole. Wherever "people" is used in such a sense, there
is always fallacy. Furthermore, you will recognize in this definition a very superficial and fallacious construction of English
constitutional history. The writer goes on to elaborate that
construction and he comes out at last with the conclusion that
"a government by the people can, in no case, become a paternal
government, since its law-makers are its mandataries and servants
carrying out its will, and not its fathers or its masters." This, then,
is the point at which he desires to arrive, and he has followed a
familiar device in setting up a definition to start with which
would produce the desired deduction at the end.

In the definition the word "people" was used for a class or
section of the population. It is now asserted that if *that* section
rules, there can be no paternal, that is, undue, government. That
doctrine, however, is the very opposite of liberty and contains
the most vicious error possible in politics. The truth is that
cupidity, selfishness, envy, malice, lust, vindictiveness are constant
vices of human nature. They are not confined to classes or to
nations or particular ages of the world. They present themselves
in the palace, in the parliament, in the academy, in the church,
in the workshop, and in the hovel. They appear in autocracies,
theocracies, aristocracies, democracies, and ochlocracies all alike.
They change their masks somewhat from age to age and from
one form of society to another. All history is only one long story
to this effect: men have struggled for power over their fellow-men
in order that they might win the joys of earth at the expense of
others and might shift the burdens of life from their own shoul-
ders upon those of others. It is true that, until this time, the
proletariat, the mass of mankind, have rarely had the power and
they have not made such a record as kings and nobles and priests
have made of the abuses they would perpetrate against their
fellow-men when they could and dared. But what folly it is to
think that vice and passion are limited by classes, that liberty
consists only in taking power away from nobles and priests and
giving it to artisans and peasants and that these latter will never
abuse it! They will abuse it just as all others have done unless
they are put under checks and guarantees, and there can be no
civil liberty anywhere unless rights are guaranteed against all

abuses, as well from proletarians as from generals, aristocrats, and ecclesiastics.

Now what has been amiss in all the old arrangements? The evils of the old military and aristocratic governments was that some men enjoyed the fruits of other men's labor; that some persons' lives, rights, interests and happiness were sacrificed to other persons' cupidity and lust. What have our ancestors been striving for, under the name of civil liberty, for the last five hundred years? They have been striving to bring it about that each man and woman might live out his or her life according to his or her own notions of happiness and up to the measure of his or her own virtue and wisdom. How have they sought to accomplish this? They have sought to accomplish it by setting aside all arbitrary personal or class elements and introducing the reign of law and the supremacy of constitutional institutions like the jury, the habeas corpus, the independent judiciary, the separation of church and state, and the ballot. Note right here one point which will be important and valuable when I come more especially to the case of the Forgotten Man: whenever you talk of liberty, you must have *two* men in mind. The sphere of rights of one of these men trenches upon that of the other, and whenever you establish liberty for the one, you repress the other. Whenever absolute sovereigns are subjected to constitutional restraints, you always hear them remonstrate that their liberty is curtailed. So it is, in the sense that their power of determining what shall be done in the state is limited below what it was before and the similar power of other organs in the state is widened. Whenever the privileges of an aristocracy are curtailed, there is heard a similar complaint. The truth is that the line of limit or demarcation between classes as regards civil power has been moved and what has been taken from one class is given to another.

We may now, then, advance a step in our conception of civil liberty. It is the status in which we find the true adjustment of rights between classes and individuals. Historically, the conception of civil liberty has been constantly changing. The notion of rights changes from one generation to another and the conception of civil liberty changes with it. If we try to formulate a true definition of civil liberty as an ideal thing towards which the development of political institutions is all the time tending, it would be this: Civil liberty is the status of the man who is guaranteed by law and civil institutions the exclusive employment of all his own powers for his own welfare.

This definition of liberty or civil liberty, you see, deals only with concrete and actual relations of the civil order. There is some sort of a poetical and metaphysical notion of liberty afloat in men's minds which some people dream about but which nobody can define. In popular language it means that a man may do as he has a mind to. When people get this notion of liberty into their heads and combine with it the notion that they live in a free country and ought to have liberty, they sometimes make strange demands upon the state. If liberty means to be able to do as you have a mind to, there is no such thing in this world. Can the Czar of Russia do as he has a mind to? Can the Pope do as he has a mind to? Can the President of the United States do as he has a mind to? Can Rothschild do as he has a mind to? Could a Humboldt or a Faraday do as he had a mind to? Could a Shakespeare or a Raphael do as he had a mind to? Can a tramp do as he has a mind to? Where is the man, whatever his station, possessions, or talents, who can get any such liberty? There is none. There is a doctrine floating about in our literature that we are born to the inheritance of certain rights. That is another glorious dream, for it would mean that there was something in this world which we got for nothing. But what is the truth? We are born into no right whatever but what has an equivalent and corresponding duty right alongside of it. There is no such thing on this earth as something for nothing. Whatever we inherit of wealth, knowledge, or institutions from the past has been paid for by the labor and sacrifice of preceding generations; and the fact that these gains are carried on, that the race lives and that the race can, at least within some cycle, accumulate its gains, is one of the facts on which civilization rests. The law of the conservation of energy is not simply a law of physics; it is a law of the whole moral universe, and the order and truth of all things conceivable by man depends upon it. If there were any such liberty as that of doing as you have a mind to, the human race would be condemned to everlasting anarchy and war as these erratic wills crossed and clashed against each other. True liberty lies in the equilibrium of rights and duties, producing peace, order, and harmony. As I have defined it, it means that a man's right to take power and wealth out of the social product is measured by the energy and wisdom which he has contributed to the social effort.

Now if I have set this idea before you with any distinctness and success, you see that civil liberty consists of a set of civil institutions and laws which are arranged to act as impersonally as possible. It does not consist in majority rule or in universal suffrage or in elective systems at all. These are devices which are good or better just in the degree in which they secure liberty. The institutions of civil liberty leave each man to run his career in life in his own way, only guaranteeing to him that whatever he does in the way of industry, economy, prudence, sound judgment, etc., shall redound to his own welfare and shall not be diverted to someone else's benefit. Of course it is a necessary corollary that each man shall also bear the penalty of his own vices and his own mistakes. If I want to be free from any other man's dictation, I must understand that I can have no other man under my control.

Now with these definitions and general conceptions in mind, let us turn to the special class of facts to which, as I said at the outset, I invite your attention. We see that under a régime of liberty and equality before the law, we get the highest possible development of independence, self-reliance, individual energy, and enterprise, but we get these high social virtues at the expense of the old sentimental ties which used to unite baron and retainer, master and servant, sage and disciple, comrade and comrade. We are agreed that the son shall not be disgraced even by the crime of the father, much less by the crime of a more distant relative. It is a humane and rational view of things that each life shall stand for itself alone and not be weighted by the faults of another, but it is useless to deny that this view of things is possible only in a society where the ties of kinship have lost nearly all the intensity of poetry and romance which once characterized them. The ties of sentiment and sympathy also have faded out. We have come, under the régime of liberty and equality before the

law, to a form of society which is based not on status, but on free
contract. Now a society based on status is one in which classes,
ranks, interests, industries, guilds, associations, etc., hold men in
permanent relations to each other. Custom and prescription
create, under status, ties, the strength of which lies in sentiment.
Feeble remains of this may be seen in some of our academical
societies to-day, and it is unquestionably a great privilege and
advantage for any man in our society to win an experience of the
sentiments which belong to a strong and close association, just
because the chances for such experience are nowadays very rare.
In a society based on free contract, men come together as free
and independent parties to an agreement which is of mutual
advantage. The relation is rational, even rationalistic. It is not
poetical. It does not exist from use and custom, but for reasons
given, and it does not endure by prescription but ceases when
the reason for it ceases. There is no sentiment in it at all. The
fact is that, under the régime of liberty and equality before the
law, there is no place for sentiment in trade or politics as public
interests. Sentiment is thrown back into private life, into personal
relations, and if ever it comes into a public discussion of an
impersonal and general public question it always produces mischief.

Now you know that "the poor and the weak" are continually
put forward as objects of public interest and public obligation. In
the appeals which are made, the terms "the poor" and "the weak"
are used as if they were terms of exact definition. Except the
pauper, that is to say, the man who cannot earn his living or
pay his way, there is no possible definition of a poor man. Except
a man who is incapacitated by vice or by physical infirmity, there
is no definition of a weak man. The paupers and the physically
incapacitated are an inevitable charge on society. About them no
more need be said. But the weak who constantly arouse the pity
of humanitarians and philanthropists are the shiftless, the imprudent, the negligent, the impractical, and the inefficient, or they
are the idle, the intemperate, the extravagant, and the vicious.
Now the troubles of these persons are constantly forced upon
public attention, as if they and their interests deserved especial
consideration, and a great portion of all organized and unorgan-

ized effort for the common welfare consists in attempts to relieve these classes of people. I do not wish to be understood now as saying that nothing ought to be done for these people by those who are stronger and wiser. That is not my point. What I want to do is to point out the thing which is overlooked and the error which is made in all these charitable efforts. The notion is accepted as if it were not open to any question that if you help the inefficient and vicious you may gain something for society or you may not, but that you lose nothing. This is a complete mistake. Whatever capital you divert to the support of a shiftless and good-for-nothing person is so much diverted from some other employment, and that means from somebody else. I would spend any conceivable amount of zeal and eloquence if I possessed it to try to make people grasp this idea. Capital is force. If it goes one way it cannot go another. If you give a loaf to a pauper you cannot give the same loaf to a laborer. Now this other man who would have got it but for the charitable sentiment which bestowed it on a worthless member of society is the Forgotten Man. The philanthropists and humanitarians have their minds all full of the wretched and miserable whose case appeals to compassion, attacks the sympathies, takes possession of the imagination, and excites the emotions. They push on towards the quickest and easiest remedies and they forget the real victim.

Now who is the Forgotten Man? He is the simple, honest laborer, ready to earn his living by productive work. We pass him by because he is independent, self-supporting, and asks no favors. He does not appeal to the emotions or excite the sentiments. He only wants to make a contract and fulfill it, with respect on both sides and favor on neither side. He must get his living out of the capital of the country. The larger the capital is, the better living he can get. Every particle of capital which is wasted on the vicious, the idle, and the shiftless is so much taken from the capital available to reward the independent and productive laborer. But we stand with our backs to the independent and productive laborer all the time. We do not remember him because he makes no clamor; but I appeal to you whether he is not the man who ought to be remembered first of all, and whether, on any sound social theory, we ought not to protect him against

the burdens of the good-for-nothing. In these last years I have
read hundreds of articles and heard scores of sermons and speeches
which were really glorifications of the good-for-nothing, as if
these were the charge of society, recommended by right reason to
its care and protection. We are addressed all the time as if those
who are respectable were to blame because some are not so, and
as if there were an obligation on the part of those who have done
their duty towards those who have not done their duty. Every
man is bound to take care of himself and his family and to do
his share in the work of society. It is totally false that one who
has done so is bound to bear the care and charge of those who
are wretched because they have not done so. The silly popular
notion is that the beggars live at the expense of the rich, but the
truth is that those who eat and produce not, live at the expense
of those who labor and produce. The next time that you are
tempted to subscribe a dollar to a charity, I do not tell you not
to do it, because after you have fairly considered the matter,
you may think it right to do it, but I do ask you to stop and
remember the Forgotten Man and understand that if you put
your dollar in the savings bank it will go to swell the capital
of the country which is available for division amongst those who,
while they earn it, will reproduce it with increase.

Let us now go on to another class of cases. There are a great
many schemes brought forward for "improving the condition of
the working classes." I have shown already that a free man cannot
take a favor. One who takes a favor or submits to patronage
demeans himself. He falls under obligation. He cannot be free
and he cannot assert a station of equality with the man who
confers the favor on him. The only exception is where there are
exceptional bonds of affection or friendship, that is, where the
sentimental relation supersedes the free relation. Therefore, in a
country which is a free democracy, all propositions to do something for the working classes have an air of patronage and
superiority which is impertinent and out of place. No one can do
anything for anybody else unless he has a surplus of energy to
dispose of after taking care of himself. In the United States, the
working classes, technically so called, are the strongest classes.
It is they who have a surplus to dispose of if anybody has. Why

should anybody else offer to take care of them or to serve them? They can get whatever they think worth having and, at any rate, if they are free men in a free state, it is ignominious and unbecoming to introduce fashions of patronage and favoritism here. A man who, by superior education and experience of business, is in a position to advise a struggling man of the wages class, is certainly held to do so and will, I believe, always be willing and glad to do so; but this sort of activity lies in the range of private and personal relations.

⌈ I now, however, desire to direct attention to the public, general, and impersonal schemes, and I point out the fact that, if you undertake to lift anybody, you must have a fulcrum or point of resistance. ⌋All the elevation you give to one must be gained by an equivalent depression on someone else. The question of gain to society depends upon the balance of the account, as regards the position of the persons who undergo the respective operations. ⌈But nearly all the schemes for "improving the condition of the working man" involve an elevation of some working men at the expense of other working men. ⌋When you expend capital or labor to elevate some persons who come within the sphere of your influence, you interfere in the conditions of competition. ⌈The advantage of some is won by an equivalent loss of others. ⌋The difference is not brought about by the energy and effort of the persons themselves. If it were, there would be nothing to be said about it, for we constantly see people surpass others in the rivalry of life and carry off the prizes which the others must do without. In the cases I am discussing, the difference is brought about by an interference which must be partial, arbitrary, accidental, controlled by favoritism and personal preference. I do not say, in this case, either, that we ought to do no work of this kind. On the contrary, I believe that the arguments for it quite outweigh, in many cases, the arguments against it. What I desire, again, is to bring out the forgotten element which we always need to remember in order to make a wise decision as to any scheme of this kind. I want to call to mind the⌈Forgotten Man, because, in this case also, if we recall him and go to look for him, we shall find him patiently and perseveringly, manfully and independently struggling against adverse circumstances without complaining or

begging. If, then, we are led to heed the groaning and complaining of others and to take measures for helping these others, we
shall, before we know it, push down this man who is trying to
help himself.

Let us take another class of cases. So far we have said nothing
about the abuse of legislation. We all seem to be under the delusion that the rich pay the taxes. Taxes are not thrown upon the
consumers with any such directness and completeness as is sometimes assumed; but that, in ordinary states of the market, taxes
on houses fall, for the most part, on the tenants and that taxes on
commodities fall, for the most part, on the consumers, is beyond
question. Now the state and municipality go to great expense to
support policemen and sheriffs and judicial officers, to protect
people against themselves, that is, against the results of their own
folly, vice, and recklessness. Who pays for it? Undoubtedly the
people who have not been guilty of folly, vice, or recklessness.
Out of nothing comes nothing. We cannot collect taxes from
people who produce nothing and save nothing. The people who
have something to tax must be those who have produced and
saved.

When you see a drunkard in the gutter, you are disgusted, but
you pity him. When a policeman comes and picks him up you are
satisfied. You say that "society" has interfered to save the drunkard from perishing. Society is a fine word, and it saves us the
trouble of thinking to say that society acts. The truth is that the
policeman is paid by somebody, and when we talk about society
we forget who it is that pays. It is the Forgotten Man again. It is
the industrious workman going home from a hard day's work,
whom you pass without noticing, who is mulcted of a percentage
of his day's earnings to hire a policeman to save the drunkard
from himself. All the public expenditure to prevent vice has the
same effect. Vice is its own curse. If we let nature alone, she cures
vice by the most frightful penalties. It may shock you to hear me
say it, but when you get over the shock, it will do you good to
think of it: a drunkard in the gutter is just where he ought to be.
Nature is working away at him to get him out of the way, just as
she sets up her processes of dissolution to remove whatever is a
failure in its line. Gambling and less mentionable vices all cure

themselves by the ruin and dissolution of their victims. Nine-tenths of our measures for preventing vice are really protective towards it, because they ward off the penalty. "Ward off," I say, and that is the usual way of looking at it; but is the penalty really annihilated? By no means. It is turned into police and court expenses and spread over those who have resisted vice. It is the Forgotten Man again who has been subjected to the penalty while our minds were full of the drunkards, spendthrifts, gamblers, and other victims of dissipation. Who is, then, the Forgotten Man? He is the clean, quiet, virtuous, domestic citizen, who pays his debts and his taxes and is never heard of out of his little circle. Yet who is there in the society of a civilized state who deserves to be remembered and considered by the legislator and statesman before this man?

Another class of cases is closely connected with this last. There is an apparently invincible prejudice in people's minds in favor of state regulation. All experience is against state regulation and in favor of liberty. The freer the civil institutions are, the more weak or mischievous state regulation is. The Prussian bureaucracy can do a score of things for the citizen which no governmental organ in the United States can do; and, conversely, if we want to be taken care of as Prussians and Frenchmen are, we must give up something of our personal liberty.

Now we have a great many well-intentioned people among us who believe that they are serving their country when they discuss plans for regulating the relations of employer and employee, or the sanitary regulations of dwellings, or the construction of factories, or the way to behave on Sunday, or what people ought not to eat or drink or smoke. All this is harmless enough and well enough as a basis of mutual encouragement and missionary enterprise, but it is almost always made a basis of legislation. The reformers want to get a majority, that is, to get the power of the state and so to make other people do what the reformers think it right and wise to do. A and B agree to spend Sunday in a certain way. They get a law passed to make C pass it in their way. They determine to be teetotallers and they get a law passed to make C be a teetotaller for the sake of D who is likely to drink too much. Factory acts for women and children are right because women and children are not on an equal footing with men and cannot, therefore, make contracts properly. Adult men, in a free state, must be left to make their own contracts and defend themselves. It will not do to say that some men are weak and unable to make contracts any better than women. Our civil institutions assume that all men are equal in political capacity and all are given equal measure of political power and right, which is not the case with women and children. If, then, we measure political rights by one theory and social responsibilities by another, we produce an immoral and vicious relation. A and B, however, get factory acts and other acts passed regulating the relation of employers and employee and set armies of commissioners and inspectors traveling about to see to things, instead of using their efforts, if any are needed, to lead the free men to make their own conditions as to what kind of factory buildings they will work in, how many hours they will work, what they will do on Sunday and so on. The consequence is that men lose the true education in freedom which is needed to support free institutions. They are taught to rely on government officers and inspectors. The whole system of government inspectors is corrupting to free institutions. In England, the liberals used always to regard state regulation with suspicion, but since they have come to power, they plainly believe that state regulation is a good thing—if *they* regulate—because, of course, they want to bring about good things. In this country each party takes turns, according as it is in or out, in supporting or denouncing the non-interference theory.

Now, if we have state regulation, what is always forgotten is this: Who pays for it? Who is the victim of it? There always is a victim. The workmen who do not defend themselves have to pay for the inspectors who defend them. The whole system of social regulation by boards, commissioners, and inspectors consists in relieving negligent people of the consequences of their negligence and so leaving them to continue negligent without correction. That system also turns away from the agencies which are close, direct, and germane to the purpose, and seeks others. Now, if you relieve negligent people of the consequences of their negligence, you can only throw those consequences on the people who have not been negligent. If you turn away from the agencies which are direct and cognate to the purpose, you can only employ other agencies. Here, then, you have your Forgotten Man again. The man who has been careful and prudent and who wants to go on and reap his advantages for himself and his children is arrested just at that point, and he is told that he must go and take care of some negligent employees in a factory or on a railroad who have not provided precautions for themselves or have not forced their employers to provide precautions, or negligent tenants who have not taken care of their own sanitary arrangements, or negligent householders who have not provided against fire, or negligent parents who have not sent their children to school. If the Forgotten Man does not go, he must hire an inspector to go. No doubt it is often worth his while to go or send, rather than leave the thing undone, on account of his remoter interest; but what I want to show is that all this is unjust to the Forgotten Man, and that the reformers and philosophers miss the point entirely when they preach that it is his duty to do all this work. Let them preach to the negligent to learn to take care of themselves. Whenever A and B put their heads together and decide what A, B and C must do for D, there is never any pressure on A and B. They consent to it and like it. There is rarely any pressure on D because he does not like it and contrives to evade it. The pressure all comes on C. Now, who is C? He is always the man who, if let alone, would make a reasonable use of his liberty without abusing it. He would not constitute any social problem at all and would not need any regulation. He is the Forgotten Man again, and as soon as he is brought from his obscurity you see that he is just that one amongst us who is what we all ought to be.

Let us look at another case. I read again and again arguments to prove that criminals have claims and rights against society. Not long ago, I read an account of an expensive establishment for the reformation of criminals, and I am told that we ought to reform criminals, not merely punish them vindictively. When I was a young man, I read a great many novels by Eugene Sue, Victor Hugo, and other Frenchmen of the school of '48, in which the badness of a bad man is represented, not as his fault, but as the fault of society. Now, as society consists of the bad men plus the good men, and as the object of this declaration was to show that the badness of the bad men was not the fault of the bad men, it remains that the badness of the bad men must be the fault of the good men. No doubt, it is far more consoling to the bad men than even to their friends to reach the point of this demonstration.

Let us ask, now, for a moment, what is the sense of punishment, since a good many people seem to be quite in a muddle about it. Every man in society is bound in nature and reason to contribute to the strength and welfare of society. He ought to work, to be peaceful, honest, just, and virtuous. [A criminal is a man who, instead of working with and for society, turns his efforts against the common welfare in some way or other. He disturbs order, violates harmony, invades the security and happiness of others, wastes and destroys capital. If he is put to death, it is on the ground that he has forfeited all right to existence in society by the magnitude of his offenses against its welfare. If he is imprisoned, it is simply a judgment of society upon him that he is so mischievous to the society that he must be segregated from it.] His punishment is a warning to him to reform himself, just exactly like the penalties inflicted by God and nature on vice. A man who has committed crime is, therefore, a burden on society and an injury to it. He is a destructive and not a productive force and everybody is worse off for his existence than if he did not exist. Whence, then, does he obtain a right to be taught or reformed at the public expense? The whole question of what to do with him is one of expediency, and it embraces the whole range of possible policies from that of execution to that of education and reformation, but when the expediency of reformatory attempts is discussed we always forget the labor and expense and who must pay. All that the state does for the criminal, beyond forcing him to earn his living, is done at the expense of the industrious member of society who never costs the state anything for correction and discipline. If a man who has gone astray can be reclaimed in any way, no one would hinder such a work, but people whose minds are full of sympathy and interest for criminals and who desire to adopt some systematic plans of reformatory efforts are only, once more, trampling on the Forgotten Man.

Let us look at another case. If there is a public office to be filled, of course a great number of persons come forward as candidates for it. Many of these persons are urged as candidates on the ground that they are badly off, or that they cannot support themselves, or that they want to earn a living while educating themselves, or that they have female relatives dependent on them, or for some other reason of a similar kind. In other cases, candidates are presented and urged on the ground of their kinship to somebody, or on account of service, it may be meritorious service, in some other line than that of the duty to be performed. Men are proposed for clerkships on the ground of service in the army twenty years ago, or for customhouse inspectors on the ground of public services in the organization of political parties. If public positions are granted on these grounds of sentiment or favoritism, the abuse is to be condemned on the ground of the harm done to the public interest; but I now desire to point out another thing which is constantly forgotten. If you give a position to A, you cannot give it to B. If A is an object of sentiment or favoritism and not a person fit and competent to fulfill the duty, who is B? He is somebody who has nothing but merit on his side, somebody who has no powerful friends, no political influence, some quiet, unobtrusive individual who has known no other way to secure the chances of life than simply to deserve them. Here we have the Forgotten Man again, and once again we find him worthy of all respect and consideration, but passed by in favor of the noisy, pushing, and incompetent. Who ever remembers that if you give a place to a man who is unfit for it you are keeping out of it somebody, somewhere, who is fit for it?

Let us take another case. A trades-union is an association of journeymen in a certain trade which has for one of its chief objects to raise wages in that trade. This object can be accomplished only by drawing more capital into the trade, or by lessening the supply of labor in it. To do the latter, the trades-unions limit the number of apprentices who may be admitted to the trade. In discussing this device, people generally fix their minds on the beneficiaries of this arrangement. It is desired by everybody that wages should be as high as they can be under the conditions of industry. Our minds are directed by the facts of the

case to the men who are in the trade already and are seeking
their own advantage. Sometimes people go on to notice the effects
of trades-unionism on the employers, but although employers are
constantly vexed by it, it is seen that they soon count it into the
risks of their business and settle down to it philosophically. Sometimes people go further then and see that, if the employer adds
the trades-union and strike risk to the other risks, he submits to
it because he has passed it along upon the public and that the
public wealth is diminished by trades-unionism, which is undoubtedly the case. I do not remember, however, that I have ever
seen in print any analysis and observation of trades-unionism
which takes into account its effect in another direction. The
effect on employers or on the public would not raise wages. The
public pays more for houses and goods, but that does not raise
wages. The surplus paid by the public is pure loss, because it is
only paid to cover an extra business risk of the employer. If
their trades-unions raise wages, how do they do it? They do it by
lessening the supply of labor in the trade, and this they do by
limiting the number of apprentices. All that is won, therefore,
for those in the trade, is won at the expense of those persons in
the same class in life who want to get into the trade but are
forbidden. Like every other monopoly, this one secures advantages for those who are in only at a greater loss to those who
are kept out. Who, then, are those who are kept out and who are
always forgotten in all the discussions? They are the Forgotten
Men again; and what kind of men are they? They are those
young men who want to earn their living by the trade in question.
Since they select it, it is fair to suppose that they are fit for it,
would succeed at it, and would benefit society by practicing it;
but they are arbitrarily excluded from it and are perhaps pushed
down into the class of unskilled laborers. When people talk of
the success of a trades-union in raising wages, they forget these
persons who have really, in a sense, paid the increase.

Let me now turn your attention to another class of cases. I
have shown how, in time past, the history of states has been a
history of selfishness, cupidity, and robbery, and I have affirmed
that now and always the problems of government are how to deal
with these same vices of human nature. People are always prone

to believe that there is something metaphysical and sentimental about civil affairs, but there is not. Civil institutions are constructed to protect, either directly or indirectly, the property of men and the honor of women against the vices and passions of human nature. In our day and country, the problem presents new phases, but it is there just the same as it ever was, and the problem is only the more difficult for us because of its new phase which prevents us from recognizing it. In fact, our people are raving and struggling against it in a kind of blind way, not yet having come to recognize it. More than half of their blows, at present, are misdirected and fail of their object, but they will be aimed better by and by. There is a great deal of clamor about watering stocks and the power of combined capital, which is not very intelligent or well-directed. The evil and abuse which people are groping after in all these denunciations is jobbery.

By jobbery I mean the constantly apparent effort to win wealth, not by honest and independent production, but by some sort of a scheme for extorting other people's product from them. A large part of our legislation consists in making a job for somebody. Public buildings are jobs, not always, but in most cases. The buildings are not needed at all or are costly far beyond what is useful or even decently luxurious. Internal improvements are jobs. They are carried out, not because they are needed in themselves, but because they will serve the turn of some private interest, often incidentally that of the very legislators who pass the appropriations for them. A man who wants a farm, instead of going out where there is plenty of land available for it, goes down under the Mississippi River to make a farm, and then wants his fellow-citizens to be taxed to dyke the river so as to keep it off his farm. The California hydraulic miners have washed the gold out of the hillsides and have washed the dirt down into the valleys to the ruin of the rivers and the farms. They want the federal government to remove this dirt at the national expense. The silver miners, finding that their product is losing value in the market, get the government to go into the market as a great buyer in the hope of sustaining the price. The national government is called upon to buy or hire unsalable ships; to dig canals which will not pay; to educate illiterates in the states which have not done their duty at the expense of the states which have done their duty as to education; to buy up telegraphs which no longer pay; and to provide the capital for enterprises of which private individuals are to win the profits. We are called upon to squander twenty millions on swamps and creeks; from twenty to sixty-six millions on the Mississippi River; one hundred millions in pensions—and there is now a demand for another hundred million beyond that. This is the great plan of all living on each other. The pensions in England used to be given to aristocrats who had political power, in order to corrupt them. Here the pensions are given to the great democratic mass who have the political power, in order to corrupt them. We have one hundred thousand federal office-holders and I do not know how many state and municipal office-holders. Of course public officers are necessary and it is an economical organization of society to set apart some of its members for civil functions, but if the number of persons drawn from production and supported by the producers while engaged in civil functions is in undue proportion to the total population, there is economic loss. If public offices are treated as spoils or benefices or sinecures, then they are jobs and only constitute part of the pillage.

The biggest job of all is a protective tariff. This device consists in delivering every man over to be plundered by his neighbor and in teaching him to believe that it is a good thing for him and his country because he may take his turn at plundering the rest. Mr. Kelley[1] said that if the internal revenue taxes on whisky and tobacco, which are paid to the United States government, were not taken off, there would be a rebellion. Just then it was discovered that Sumatra tobacco was being imported, and the Connecticut tobacco men hastened to Congress to get a tax laid on it for their advantage. So it appears that if a tax is laid on tobacco, to be paid to the United States, there will be a rebellion, but if a tax is laid on it to be paid to the farmers of the Connecticut Valley, there will be no rebellion at all. The tobacco farmers having been taxed for protected manufactures are now to be taken into the system, and the workmen in the factories are to be

[1] William Darrah "Pig Iron" Kelley (1814-1890), Pennsylvania Republican, was the leading advocate of a high protective tariff in Congress. [S. P.]

taxed on their tobacco to protect the farmers. So the system is rendered more complete and comprehensive.

On every hand you find this jobbery. The government is to give every man a pension, and every man an office, and every man a tax to raise the price of his product, and to clean out every man's creek for him, and to buy all his unsalable property, and to provide him with plenty of currency to pay his debts, and to educate his children, and to give him the use of a library and a park and a museum and a gallery of pictures. On every side the doors of waste and extravagance stand open; and spend, squander, plunder, and grab are the watchwords. We grumble some about it and talk about the greed of corporations and the power of capital and the wickedness of stock gambling. Yet we elect the legislators who do all this work. Of course, we should never think of blaming ourselves for electing men to represent and govern us, who, if I may use a slang expression, give us away. What man ever blamed himself for his misfortune? We groan about monopolies and talk about more laws to prevent the wrongs done by chartered corporations. Who made the charters? Our representatives. Who elected such representatives? We did. How can we get bad law-makers to make a law which shall prevent bad law-makers from making a bad law? That is, really, what we are trying to do. If we are a free, self-governing people, all our misfortunes come right home to ourselves and we can blame nobody else. Is anyone astonished to find that men are greedy, whether they are incorporated or not? Is it a revelation to find that we need, in our civil affairs, to devise guarantees against selfishness, rapacity, and fraud? I have ventured to affirm that government has never had to deal with anything else.

Now, I have said that this jobbery means waste, plunder, and loss, and I defined it at the outset as the system of making a chance to extort part of his product from somebody else. Now comes the question: Who pays for it all? The system of plundering each other soon destroys all that it deals with. It produces nothing. Wealth comes only from production, and all that the wrangling grabbers, loafers, and jobbers get to deal with comes from somebody's toil and sacrifice. Who, then, is he who provides it all? Go and find him and you will have once more before you

the Forgotten Man. You will find him hard at work because he
has a great many to support. Nature has done a great deal for
him in giving him a fertile soil and an excellent climate and he
wonders why it is that, after all, his scale of comfort is so
moderate. He has to get out of the soil enough to pay all his
taxes, and that means the cost of all the jobs and the fund for all
the plunder. The Forgotten Man is delving away in patient industry, supporting his family, paying his taxes, casting his vote,
supporting the church and the school, reading his newspaper,
and cheering for the politician of his admiration, but he is the
only one for whom there is no provision in the great scramble and
the big divide.

Such is the Forgotten Man. He works, he votes, generally he
prays—but he always pays—yes, above all, he pays. He does not
want an office; his name never gets into the newspaper except
when he gets married or dies. He keeps production going on. He
contributes to the strength of parties. He is flattered before election. He is strongly patriotic. He is wanted, whenever, in his little
circle, there is work to be done or counsel to be given. He may
grumble some occasionally to his wife and family, but he does
not frequent the grocery or talk politics at the tavern. Consequently, he is forgotten. He is a commonplace man. He gives no
trouble. He excites no admiration. He is not in any way a hero
(like a popular orator); or a problem (like tramps and outcasts);
nor notorious (like criminals); nor an object of sentiment (like
the poor and weak); nor a burden (like paupers and loafers); nor
an object out of which social capital may be made (like the
beneficiaries of church and state charities); nor an object for
charitable aid and protection (like animals treated with cruelty);
nor the object of a job (like the ignorant and illiterate); nor one
over whom sentimental economists and statesmen can parade
their fine sentiments (like inefficient workmen and shiftless
artisans). Therefore, he is forgotten. All the burdens fall on him,
or on her, for it is time to remember that the Forgotten Man is
not seldom a woman.

When you go to Willimantic, they will show you with great
pride the splendid thread mills there. I am told that there are
sewing-women who can earn only fifty cents in twelve hours, and

provide the thread. In the cost of every spool of thread more than one cent is tax. It is paid, not to get the thread, for you could get the thread without it. It is paid to get the Willimantic linen company which is not worth having and which is, in fact, a nuisance, because it makes thread harder to get than it would be if there were no such concern. If a woman earns fifty cents in twelve hours, she earns a spool of thread as nearly as may be in an hour, and if she uses a spool of thread per day, she works a quarter of an hour per day to support the Willimantic linen company, which in 1882 paid 95 per cent dividend to its stockholders. If you go and look at the mill, it will captivate your imagination until you remember all the women in all the garrets, and all the artisans' and laborers' wives and children who are spending their hours of labor, not to get goods which they need, but to pay for the industrial system which only stands in their way and makes it harder for them to get the goods.

It is plain enough that the Forgotten Man and the Forgotten Woman are the very life and substance of society. They are the ones who ought to be first and always remembered. They are always forgotten by sentimentalists, philanthropists, reformers, enthusiasts, and every description of speculator in sociology, political economy, or political science. If a student of any of these sciences ever comes to understand the position of the Forgotten Man and to appreciate his true value, you will find such student an uncompromising advocate of the strictest scientific thinking on all social topics, and a cold and hard-hearted skeptic towards all artificial schemes of social amelioration. If it is desired to bring about social improvements, bring us a scheme for relieving the Forgotten Man of some of his burdens. He is our productive force which we are wasting. Let us stop wasting his force. Then we shall have a clean and simple gain for the whole society. The Forgotten Man is weighted down with the cost and burden of the schemes for making everybody happy, with the cost of public beneficence, with the support of all the loafers, with the loss of all the economic quackery, with the cost of all the jobs. Let us remember him a little while. Let us take some of the burdens off him. Let us turn our pity on him instead of on the good-for-nothing. It will be only justice to him, and society will greatly

gain by it. Why should we not also have the satisfaction of thinking and caring for a little while about the clean, honest, industrious, independent, self-supporting men and women who have
not inherited much to make life luxurious for them, but who are
doing what they can to get on in the world without begging from
anybody, especially since all they want is to be let alone, with good
friendship and honest respect. Certainly the philanthropists and
sentimentalists have kept our attention for a long time on the
nasty, shiftless, criminal, whining, crawling, and good-for-nothing
people, as if they alone deserved our attention.

The Forgotten Man is never a pauper. He almost always has a
little capital because it belongs to the character of the man to
save something. He never has more than a little. He is, therefore, poor in the popular sense, although in the correct sense he
is not so. I have said already that if you learn to look for the
Forgotten Man and to care for him, you will be very skeptical
toward all philanthropic and humanitarian schemes. It is clear
now that the interest of the Forgotten Man and the interest of
"the poor," "the weak," and the other petted classes are in
antagonism. In fact, the warning to you to look for the Forgotten Man comes the minute that the orator or writer begins to
talk about the poor man. That minute the Forgotten Man is
in danger of a new assault, and if you intend to meddle in the
matter at all, then is the minute for you to look about for him
and to give him your aid. Hence, if you care for the Forgotten
Man, you will be sure to be charged with *not* caring for the poor.
Whatever you do for any of the petted classes wastes capital. If
you do anything for the Forgotten Man, you must secure him his
earnings and savings, that is, you legislate for the security of
capital and for its free employment; you must oppose paper
money, wildcat banking and usury laws and you must maintain
the inviolability of contracts. Hence you must be prepared to be
told that you favor the capitalist class, the enemy of the poor
man.

What the Forgotten Man really wants is true liberty. Most of his
wrongs and woes come from the fact that there are yet mixed
together in our institutions the old mediæval theories of protection and personal dependence and the modern theories of in-

dependence and individual liberty. The consequence is that the people who are clever enough to get into positions of control, measure their own rights by the paternal theory and their own duties by the theory of independent liberty. It follows that the Forgotten Man, who is hard at work at home, has to pay both ways. His rights are measured by the theory of liberty, that is, he has only such as he can conquer. His duties are measured by the paternal theory, that is, he must discharge all which are laid upon him, as is always the fortune of parents. People talk about the paternal theory of government as if it were a very simple thing. Analyze it, however, and you see that in every paternal relation there must be two parties, a parent and a child, and when you speak metaphorically, it makes all the difference in the world who is parent and who is child. Now, since we, the people, are the state, whenever there is any work to be done or expense to be paid, and since the petted classes and the criminals and the jobbers cost and do not pay, it is they who are in the position of the child, and it is the Forgotten Man who is the parent. What the Forgotten Man needs, therefore, is that we come to a clearer understanding of liberty and to a more complete realization of it. Every step which we win in liberty will set the Forgotten Man free from some of his burdens and allow him to use his powers for himself and for the commonwealth.

VIII

Democracy and Plutocracy

One of the most difficult things to learn in social science is
that every action inside of the social organism is attended by a
reaction, and that this reaction may be spread far through the
organism, affecting organs and modifying functions which are, at
the first view of the matter, apparently so remote that they could
not be affected at all. It is a more simple statement of the same
fact to say that everything in the social organism displaces everything else. Therefore, if we set to work to interfere in the operation of the organism, with our attention all absorbed in one set of
phenomena, and regulate our policy with a view to those
phenomena only, we are very sure to do mischief. The current
speculation about social policy and social reform suffer very
largely from this error.

The organization of a modern civilized society is intensely high;
its parts are extremely complicated. Their relations with each
other are close, and all the tendencies of our time are making
them closer; and the closer they are, the more surely and im-
mediately are interferences distributed through them. The bonds
of connection between them are constantly becoming more delicate and subtle; and they are sublimated, as it were, so that they
escape the observation of the senses. In a simple society, even
though it be on the height of the best civilization, all the parts of
the organization lie bare to view, and every one can see the
relations of agriculturist, transporter, banker, merchant, profes-

sional man, debtor, creditor, employer, and employee, in their
visible operation. In a highly organized society as, for instance,
in a big city, those same relations have all become automatic
and impersonal. They have escaped from control; they are regulated by assumptions and understandings that every one is to do
so and so; that certain uniform and constant motives, aims, and
desires will present themselves as long as human society endures;
and that men will, therefore, continue to exert themselves in a
certain manner for the satisfaction of their wants. This is what
we mean by natural law, and by the field of a science of society.
If any one will look over his dinner table the next time he sits
down to dinner, he can see the proofs that thousands of producers, transporters, merchants, bankers, policemen, and me-
chanics, through the whole organization of society and all over
the globe, have been at work for the last year or more to put that
dinner within his reach, on the assumption that he, too, would
do his work in the organization, whatever it is, and be prepared
to pay for the dinner when it reaches him. All these thousands
and millions of people, therefore, have cooperated with each
other for the common good of all, without acquaintance or conventional agreement, and without any personal interest in each
other, under the play of forces which lie in human nature and
in the conditions of human existence on this earth.

Now, the organs of society do not impinge upon each other
with hard and grating friction, like blocks of granite wedged
together. If they did the case would be easier, for then we should
have only a mechanical contact, and the relations would be of a
simple order. Neither are the relations those of an orchestra,
which produces harmony by voluntary cooperation under training, according to a predetermined scheme, yet subject to the
laws of harmony in sound. Nor are the relations like those of an
army, where the cooperation is arbitrary, and enforced by
discipline, although controlled by expediency for the attainment
of an end under set conditions. The organs are elastic and they
are plastic. They suffer both temporary and permanent modifications in form and function by their interaction on each other,
and by the arbitrary interferences to which they are subjected
by legislation or artifice of any kind. Thus, for instance, it is

impossible to say how taxes will diffuse themselves; they may force a change in the immediate organ on which they fall—transporters, merchants, bankers—or they may be transmitted more or less through the organization.

It is this elasticity and plasticity of the organs of society which give the social tinker his chance, and make him think that there are no laws of the social order, no science of society; no limits, in fact, to the possibilities of manipulation by "The State."

He is always operating on the limit of give and take between the organs; he regards all the displacement which he can accomplish as positively new creation; he does not notice at all, and probably is not trained to perceive, the reaction—the other side of the change; he does not understand that he must endure a change on one side for all the change which he affects on the other. Since it is so hard to learn that exchange means exchange, and therefore has two sides to it, a giving and a taking—since, I say it is so hard to learn this, and people talk even about buying and selling as if they were independent operations, a fallacy which is itself the outcome of a high organization with a money system—then it is not strange that it should be so hard to learn that all social change is change, has two sides to it—the cost and the gain, the price and the product, the sacrifice and the obtainment.

Hence we see one fallacy of nearly all the popular propositions of "reform": they would not be amiss, perhaps, if the change which they propose could be made and everything else remain the same.

In the proposition it is assumed that everything else is to remain the same. But it is inevitable that other things will not remain the same; they will all of them adjust themselves to the new elements which are introduced. If we make a change involving expense, taxes must be increased, and every taxed interest must undergo a change to fit it to the new conditions. I know of no reform by state agency which does not involve increased taxation.

Let us note another fact. In the advancing organization of society, the tendency is all the time to subdivide the functions, and each one is assumed by a different set of persons; thus the interests of living men and women become enlisted in all the play of the organs, and are at stake in all the legislative and other interferences. What I have called the elasticity and plasticity of the organs means in fact the rights, interest, happiness, and prosperity of the one set of human beings versus the same interests of another set of human beings. It is men who strive, and suffer, and plan, and fight, and steal, and kill, when the great impersonal and automatic forces push them up against each other, or push group against group. The tendency is all the time to go back from the industrial struggle to the military struggle. Every strike illustrates it. Better educated people, while talking about respect for law, seize upon legislation as the modern mode of pursuing the military struggle under the forms of peace and order—that is to say, they turn from industrial competition and industrial effort to legislative compulsion, and to arbitrary advantages won and secured through the direction and the power of the state. When the strikers and Knights of Labor declare that they are going to reach after this power, they have simply determined to contend for the latest form of force by which to supersede the industrial struggle for existence by a struggle of craft and physical force. Yet there are those who tell us that this is really a supersession of the struggle for existence by intelligence and "ethical" forces, as if every page of the Congressional Record did not reveal the sordidness of the plans and motives by which it is all controlled.

Here comes in another fallacy in the philosophy of state interference. Let the reader note for himself with what naïveté the advocate of interference takes it for granted that he and his associates will have the administration of their legislative device in their own hands and will be sure of guiding it for their purposes only. They never appear to remember that the device, when once set up, will itself become the prize of a struggle; that it will serve one set of purposes as well as another, so that after all the only serious question is: who will get it? Here is another ground for a general and sweeping policy of non-interference. Although you may be in possession of the power of the state to-day, and it might suit you very well, either to triumph over your business rivals and competitors; or to bend to your will the social organ

which stands next to you, and with which you have the most friction (as, for instance, shippers with transporters); or to see your
pet reform (temperance, for instance) marching on, you would far
better consent to forego your satisfaction, lest presently your
rivals, or the railroads, or the liquor-sellers, should beat you in a
political struggle; and then you must suffer wrong and in the
end be forced to give up industrial and persuasive methods altogether and devote your whole energy to the political struggle,
as that on which all the rest depends.

Of all that I have here said, the Interstate Commerce Law is
the instance which stands out in point with the greatest distinctness. The shippers and transporters, the competing railroads, the
people who can extort passes and those who do not want to give
them, the people at way-stations and those at competing points,
and other interests also which cluster about the transportation,
which is the most important element in the opening up of this
great and rich continent, all clash and struggle for shares in the
wealth which the people of the United States produce. The
contest has phases and vicissitudes of every description. The
politicians, editors, economists, *littérateurs,* lawyers, labor agita-
tors, and countless others who, in one way or another, have something to make out of it join in the struggle, taking sides with the
principal parties, or hovering around the strife for what may
turn up in it. When once the fatal step is taken of invoking
legislation, the contest is changed in its character and in its arena.
That is all that is accomplished; from that time on the questions
are: Who will get this legislative power? Which interest or coali-
tion of interests (such as passed the bill) will get this, the decisive
position in the battle, under its control? Already, in some of the
Western States, the next phase has developed itself. The majority
interest, by numbers, seizes the power of the state and proceeds
to realize its own interest against all others in the most ruthless
fashion. That capital has means of defense is unquestionable;
that it will defend itself is certain; that it cannot defend itself
without resorting to all the vices of plutocracy seems inevitable.
Thus the issue of democracy and plutocracy, numbers against
capital, is made up. It is the issue which menaces modern society,
and which is destined to dispel the dreams which have been

cherished, that we were on the eve of a millennium. On the contrary, it will probably appear that the advance of civilization constantly brings new necessity for a still more elevated activity of reason and conscience, and does not tend at all to a condition of stability, in which the social and political problems of the race would reach a definitive solution.

All the words in -ocracy properly describe political forms according to the chief spring of political power in them: an autocracy is a political form in which the predominant force is the will of the monarch himself; an aristocracy is a form in which the predominant and controlling force is the will of a limited body, having the possession of the qualities which are most esteemed and envied in that society; a theocracy is a form in which the predominant force is some conception of God and his will, and, inasmuch as the will of God can come to men only through some finite channel, a theocracy easily passes into a hierocracy, in which the predominant force is possessed and wielded by a priesthood; a bureaucracy is a form in which the ultimate control of things political lies in the hands of a body of office-holders. In each case the name designates that organ which, upon ultimate analysis, is found to have the power to say what shall be and what shall not be.

A democracy, then, is a political form in which the ultimate power lies with the *demos,* the people. This mass, however, while unorganized, could not express its will or administer the affairs of the state; there has never been any state organized on such a plan. The *demos,* for political purposes, has always excluded women, minors, resident aliens, slaves, paupers, felons, etc., according to the constitution in each case; the "people," therefore, has always meant some defined section of the population, not the whole of it. Furthermore, in any modern state, even a superficial study of the current phrases and accepted formulæ will show that the word "people" is used in a technical sense to mean, not even the whole body of legal voters, but a limited number of them. A writer who rages at the idea that there are any "classes" will, in the next paragraph, reiterate all the current formulæ about the "people," and reveal by the context that he means to distinguish the people as peasants, artisans, and uneducated persons, from the rich, the educated, and the banking, mercantile, and professional classes.

Yet the current dogmas about the rights and wisdom of the people have no truth whatever, and no moral beauty, except when they are affirmed of the whole population, without any exception whatever. The dogmas in question are not really maxims or principles of actual political life and administration; they are sublime conceptions of the undeveloped power of growth and civilization in human society. As inspiring ideals, as educational motives, as moral incentives, they have incalculable value; but then they are philosophical and academical generalities, not every-day rules of action for specific exigencies. When they are once dragged down into the mud of practical politics, and are cut to the measure of party tactics, they are most pernicious falsehoods.

For instance, the notion that a human society, acting as a whole, bringing its reason and conscience to bear on its problems, traditions, and institutions, constantly reviewing its inherited faiths, examining its experiments, profiting by its own blunders, reaching out after better judgment and correcting its prejudices, can, in the sweep of time, arrive at the best conclusions as to what is socially true and wise and just, that man can get on earth, is a grand conception, and it is true. If the doctrine that the people ought to rule, and that the people know what is wise and right means this, it is true and fruitful. It will be noticed, however, that this doctrine implies that the people are to embrace every element in the society, including all the women and children, for in no sense could this grand consensus be true unless it was universal. It is of its very essence that the whole voice should be in it; it is its catholicity which constitutes its guarantee. If the feminine element is left out of it, its guarantee is gone; it is one-sided and imperfect; it is no longer human and social; it has sunk from the grade of a grand and inspiring conception to that of the party cry of a dominant interest. Neither is it true if the children are left out of it, for it is only in the sweep of time, after long and patient revision, that the judgments have authority. It must therefore be the work of generations to make those judgments; it is only the undying society, in its continuity and undistinguished generations, which can make them, and if they are to be true, the fire and hope of youth are as essential components as the inertness and conservatism of age.

Now, however, turn this same dogma into a maxim that peasants and artisans are the "people," that they are the depositaries of social and political wisdom, as distinguished from the sages and philosophers. Tell the young man not to worry about learning, to sneer at culture, to spend his nights on the street and his Sundays reading dime novels and the *Police Gazette,* and, when election day comes, to throw his vote so as to make a political job for himself or his friend; tell him that this is what is meant by the doctrine that the people ought to rule, and that in doing all this he will be uttering the oracles of political wisdom —then the great doctrine has turned into one of the most grotesque and mischievous falsehoods ever imagined.

In practice, therefore, democracy means that all those who are once admitted to political power are equal and that the power lies with the numerical majority of these equal units. If then the political divisions form themselves class-wise, then the most numerous class becomes the *demos* and is the depositary of political power. For this reason if we establish a democracy and then set the classes and the masses against each other, it is the utmost treason against democracy, because it ingrafts upon it from the start the worst vices of social discord and social greed which have disgraced the older political forms.

A plutocracy is a political form in which the real controlling force is wealth. This is the thing which seems to me to be really new and really threatening; there have been states in which there have been large plutocratic elements, but none in which wealth seemed to have such absorbing and controlling power as it threatens us. The most recent history of the civilized states of Western Europe has shown constant and rapid advance of plutocracy. The popular doctrines of the last hundred years have spread the notion that everybody ought to enjoy comfort and luxury—that luxury is a sort of right. Therefore if anybody has luxury while others have it not, this is held to prove that men have not equally shared in the fruits of civilization, and that the state in which such a condition of things exists has failed to perform its function; the next thing to do is to get hold of the state and make it perform its function of guaranteeing comfort and physical well-being to all. In the mean time, with the increasing thirst for luxury and the habit of thinking of it as within the scope of every man's right, the temptations of dishonest gain increase, and especially are all those forms of gain which come, not from defalcation and theft, but from the ingenious use of political opportunities, put under a special code by themselves. A man who is "on the make," to use a slang phrase produced from the very phenomena to which I refer, does not think of himself as dishonest, but only as a man of the world. He is only utilizing the chances which he can get or make to win gain from the conjuncture of political and social circumstances, without intentional crime such as the statute has forbidden. This runs all the way from the man who sells his vote to the statesman who abuses official power, and it produces a class of men who have their price.

The principle of plutocracy is that money buys whatever the owner of money wants, and the class just described are made to be its instruments. At the same time the entire industrial development of the modern world has been such as to connect industry with political power in the matter of joint-stock companies, corporations, franchises, concessions, public contracts, and so on, in new ways and in great magnitude. It is also to be noted that the impersonal and automatic methods of modern industry, and the fact that the actual superintendent is often a representative and quasi-trustee for others, has created the corporate conscience. An ambitious Roman used to buy and bribe his way through all the inferior magistracies up to the consulship, counting upon getting a province at last out of which he could extort enough to recoup himself, pay all his debts, and have a fortune besides. Modern plutocrats buy their way through elections and legislatures, in the confidence of being able to get powers which will recoup them for all the outlay and yield an ample surplus besides.

What I have said here about the venality of the humbler sets of people, and about the greed and arrogance of plutocrats, must not be taken to apply any further than it does apply, and the facts are to be taken only as one's knowledge will warrant. I am discussing forces and tendencies, and the magnitude attained as yet by those forces and tendencies ought not to be exaggerated. I regard plutocracy, however, as the most sordid and debasing form of political energy known to us. In its motive, its processes, its code, and its sanctions it is infinitely corrupting to all the institutions which ought to preserve and protect society. The time to recognize it for what it is, in its spirit and tendency, is when it is in its germ, not when it is full green.

Here, then, in order to analyze plutocracy further, we must make some important distinctions. Plutocracy ought to be carefully distinguished from "the power of capital." The effect of the uncritical denunciations of capital, and monopoly, and trust, of which we hear so much, is, as I shall try to show further on, to help forward plutocracy.

Not every rich man is a plutocrat. In the classical nations it was held that the pursuits of commerce and industry were degrading to the free man; and as for commerce, it was believed that every merchant was necessarily a cheat, that he must practice tricks from the necessity of the case, and that a certain ever-active craftiness and petty deceit were the traits of character in which his occupation educated him. As for the handicrafts, it was argued that they distorted a man's body and absorbed his mind and time, so that he was broken in spirit, ignorant, and sordid. The same ideas as to commerce and, in part, as to handicrafts, prevailed through the Middle Ages.

The classical civilization was built upon human slave power. For that reason it exhausted itself—consumed itself. It reached a climax of organization and development, and then began to waste capital and use up its materials and processes. It is, however, clear that any high civilization must be produced and sustained by an adequate force. In the case just mentioned it was human nerve and muscle. Now, modern civilization is based on capital, that is, on tools and machines, which subjugate natural forces and make them do the drudgery. It is this fact which has emancipated slaves and serfs, set the mass of mankind free from the drudgery which distorts the body and wears out the mind, at the same time producing a high civilization and avoiding the wear and tear on men.

The "dignity of labor" and the "power of capital" are therefore both products of the same modern movement. They go together; it is the power of capital which has made labor cease to be servile; it is the power of capital which has set women free from the drudgery of the grain-mill and the spinning-room; it is the power of capital which has enabled modern men to carry on mining and quarrying without misery, although in the classical times those forms of labor were so crushing that only the worst criminals or the lowest order of slaves were condemned to them. Every high civilization is unnatural, inasmuch as it is the product of art and effort. It is, therefore, unstable—ready to fall again to the original level, if the force and intelligence by which it is produced and maintained should fail. Our civilization is supported by capital and by modern science; if either of these fail—if we exhaust our capital, or if our science is not adequate to the tasks which fall upon it, our civilization will decline.

The dignity of capital is correlative with the dignity of labor. The capitalist has not simply fallen under the ban from which the laborer has escaped; the modern times have produced classes of men, masters of industry and accumulators of capital, who are among the most distinct and peculiar products of modern times. At what other epoch in history has any such class of men existed? There have, in earlier times, been great merchants, who have shown that the notion of a merchant as a man who cheats in weights and bets on differences, is a contemptible and ignorant calumny; the great masters of industry, however, are something entirely modern, and the vituperation of such a class as parasites, plunderers, speculators, and monopolists, is as ignorant and inexcusable as the older misconceptions of laborers which have gone out of fashion. A great capitalist is no more necessarily a plutocrat than a great general is a tyrant.

A plutocrat is a man who, having the possession of capital, and having the power of it at his disposal, uses it, not industrially, but politically; instead of employing laborers, he enlists lobbyists. Instead of applying capital to land, he operates upon the market by legislation, by artificial monopoly, by legislative privileges; he creates jobs, and erects combinations, which are half political and half industrial; he practices upon the industrial vices, makes an engine of venality, expends his ingenuity, not on processes of production, but on "knowledge of men," and on the tactics of the lobby. The modern industrial system gives him a magnificent field, one far more profitable, very often, than that of legitimate industry.

I submit, then, that it is of the utmost importance that we should recognize the truth about capital and capitalists, so as to reject the flood of nonsense and abuse which is afloat about both; that we should distinguish between the false and the true, the good and the bad, and should especially form a clear idea of the social political enemy as distinguished from everybody else. The recent history of every civilized state in the world shows the advance of plutocracy, and its injurious effects upon political institutions. The abuse and the vice, as usual, lie close beside the necessary and legitimate institution. Combinations of capital are indispensable, because we have purposes to accomplish which can be attained in no other way; monopolies exist in nature, and, however much modified by art, never cease to have their effect. Speculation is a legitimate function in the organization, and not an abuse or a public wrong. Trusts, although the name is a mistake, are evidently increasing in number all over the world, and are in great measure a result of the modern means of communication, which have made it possible for persons having a common interest, although scattered over the earth, if their number is not too great, to form combinations for the exploitation of a natural monopoly. What is gained by uncritical denunciation of these phenomena, or by indiscriminate confusion of definitions? The only effect of such procedure will be to nourish the abuses and destroy the utilities.

The first impulse is, when a social or industrial phenomenon presents itself, which is not considered good or pleasant, to say that we must pass a law against it. If plutocracy is an abuse of legislation and of political institutions, how can legislation do away with it? The trouble is that the political institutions are not strong enough to resist plutocracy; how then can they conquer plutocracy? Democracy especially dreads plutocracy, and with good reason.

There is no form of political power which is so ill-fitted to cope with plutocracy as democracy. Democracy has a whole set of institutions which are extra-legal, but are the most powerful elements in it; they are the party organization, the primary, the convention, etc. All this apparatus is well adapted to the purposes of plutocracy: it has to do with the formative stage of political activity; it is very largely operated in secret; it has a large but undefined field of legitimate, or quasi-legitimate, expenditure, for which there is no audit. As the operations of this apparatus are extra-legal they are irresponsible, yet they reach out to, and control, the public and civil functions. Even on the field of constitutional institutions, plutocracy always comes into the contest with a small body, a strong organization, a powerful motive, a definite purpose, and a strict discipline, while on the other side is a large and unorganized body, without discipline, with its ideas undefined, its interests illy understood, with an indefinite good intention.

If legislation is applied to the control of interests, especially when the latter are favored by the facts of the situation, the only effect is to impose on the interests more crafty and secret modes of action. Mr. Adams[1] says that, since the Interstate Commerce Law was passed, the methods of railroad men have become more base and more secret than ever before. The legislator, in further efforts to succeed in his undertaking, can only sacrifice more of the open and honest rights which are within his reach, just as the Russian Government, in trying to reach the discontented elements in its society, and crush them by severity, only puts honest people to unlimited inconvenience and loss, but does not catch the Nihilists. Under a democracy, when the last comes to the last, the contest between numbers and wealth is nothing but a contest between two sets of lawyers, one drawing Acts in behalf of the state, and the other devising means of defeating those Acts in

---

[1] Charles Francis Adams (1835-1915), the grandson of President John Quincy Adams, was a noted authority on the railroads who served as one of the first Railroad Commissioners in Massachusetts and later headed the Union Pacific Railroad. [S. P.]

behalf of their clients. The latter set is far better paid in consideration, in security, and in money.

I therefore maintain that this is a lamentable contest, in which all that we hold dear, speaking of public interests, is at stake, and that the wise policy in regard to it is to minimize to the utmost the relations of the state to industry. As long as there are such relations, every industrial interest is forced more or less to employ plutocratic methods. The corruption is greater, perhaps, on those who exercise them than on the objects of them. *Laissez-faire,* instead of being what it appears to be in most of the current discussions, cuts to the very bottom of the morals, the politics, and the political economy of the most important public questions of our time.

IX

The Concentration of Wealth:
Its Economic Justification

The concentration of wealth I understand to include the aggregation of wealth into large masses and its concentration under the control of a few. In this sense the concentration of wealth is indispensable to the successful execution of the tasks which devolve upon society in our time. Every task of society requires the employment of capital, and involves an economic problem in the form of the most expedient application of material means to ends. Two features most prominently distinguish the present age from all which have preceded it: first, the great scale on which all societal undertakings must be carried out; and second, the transcendent importance of competent management, that is, of the personal element in direction and control.

I speak of "societal undertakings" because it is important to notice that the prevalent modes and forms are not confined to industrial undertakings, but are universal in all the institutions and devices which have for their purpose the satisfaction of any wants of society. A modern church is a congeries of institutions which seeks to nourish good things and repress evil ones; it has buildings, apparatus, a store of supplies, a staff of employees, and a treasury. A modern church (parish) will soon be as complex a system of institutions as a mediæval monastery was. Contrast such an establishment with the corresponding one of fifty years ago. A university now needs an immense "concentration of wealth" for its outfit and work. It is as restricted in its work as the corresponding institution of fifty years ago was, although it may command twenty times as much capital and revenue. Furthermore, when we see that all these and other societal institutions pay far higher salaries to executive officers than to workers, we must recognize the fact that the element of personal executive ability is in command of the market, and that means that it is the element which decides success. To a correct understanding of our subject it is essential to recognize the concentration of wealth and control as a universal societal phenomenon, not merely as a matter of industrial power, or social sentiment, or political policy.

Stated in the concisest terms, the phenomenon is that of a more perfect integration of all societal functions. The concentration of power (wealth), more dominant control, intenser discipline, and stricter methods are but modes of securing more perfect integration. When we perceive this we see that the concentration of wealth is but one feature of a grand step in societal evolution.

Some may admit that the concentration of wealth is indispensable, but may desire to distinguish between joint-stock aggregations on the one side and individual fortunes on the other. This distinction is a product of the current social prejudice and is not valid. The predominance of the individual and personal element in control is seen in the tendency of all joint-stock enterprises to come under the control of very few persons. Every age is befooled by the notions which are in fashion in it. Our age is befooled by "democracy"; we hear arguments about the industrial organization which are deductions from democratic dogmas or which appeal to prejudice by using analogies drawn from democracy to affect sentiment about industrial relations. Industry may be republican; it never can be democratic, so long as men differ in productive power and in industrial virtue. In our time joint-stock companies, which are in form republican, are drifting over into oligarchies or monarchies because one or a few get greater efficiency of control and greater vigor of administration. They direct the enterprise in a way which produces more, or more economically. This is the purpose for which the organization exists and success in it outweighs everything else. We see the competent men refuse to join in the enterprise, unless they can control it, and we see the stockholders willingly put their property into the hands of those who are, as they think, competent to manage it successfully. The strongest and most effective organizations for industrial purposes which are formed nowadays are those of a few great capitalists, who have great personal confidence in each other and who can bring together adequate means for whatever they desire to do. Some such nucleus of individuals controls all the great joint-stock companies.

It is obvious that "concentration of wealth" can never be anything but a relative term. Between 1820 and 1830 Stephen Girard was a proverb for great wealth; to-day a man equally rich would not be noticed in New York for his wealth. In 1848 John Jacob Astor stood alone in point of wealth; to-day a great number surpass him. A fortune of $300,000 was then regarded as constituting wealth; it was taken as a minimum above which men were "rich." It is certain that before long some man will have a billion. It is impossible to criticize such a moving notion. The concentration of capital is also necessarily relative to the task to be performed; we wondered lately to see a corporation formed which had a capital of a billion. No one will wonder at such a corporation twenty-five years hence.

There seems to be a great readiness in the public mind to take alarm at these phenomena of growth—there might rather seem to be reason for public congratulation. We want to be provided with things abundantly and cheaply; that means that we want increased economic power. All these enterprises are efforts to satisfy that want, and they promise to do it. The public seems to turn especially to the politician to preserve it from the captain of industry; but when has anybody ever seen a politician who was a match for a captain of industry? One of the latest phenomena is a competition of the legislatures of several states for the profit of granting acts of incorporation; this competition consists, of course, in granting greater and greater powers and exacting less and less responsibility.

It is not my duty in this place to make a judicial statement of the good and ill of the facts I mention—I leave to others to suggest the limitations and safeguards which are required. It is enough to say here that of course all power is liable to abuse; if anybody is dreaming about a millennial state of society in which all energy will be free, yet fully controlled by paradisaic virtue, argument with him is vain. If we want results we must get control of adequate power, and we must learn to use it with safeguards. If we want to make tunnels, and to make them rapidly, we have to concentrate supplies of dynamite; danger results; we minimize it, but we never get rid of it. In late years our streets have been filled with power-driven cars and vehicles; the risk and danger of going on the streets has been very greatly increased; the danger is licensed by law, and it is inseparable from the satisfaction of our desire to move about rapidly. It is in this light that we should view the evils (if there are any) from the concentration of wealth. I do not say that "he who desires the end desires the means," because I do not believe that that dictum is true; but he who will not forego the end must be patient with the incidental ills which attend the means. It is ridiculous to attempt to reach the end while making war on the means. In matters of societal policy the problem always is to use the means and reach the end as well as possible under the conditions. It is proper to propose checks and safeguards, but an onslaught on the concentration of wealth is absurd and a recapitulation of its "dangers" is idle.

In fact, there is a true correlation between (a) the great productiveness of modern industry and the consequent rapid accumulation of capital from one period of production to another and (b) the larger and larger aggregations of capital which are required by modern industry from one period of production to another. We see that the movement is constantly accelerated, that its scope is all the time widening, and that the masses of material with which it deals are greater and greater. The dominant cause of all this is the application of steam and electricity to transportation, and the communication of intelligence—things which we boast about as great triumphs of the nineteenth century. They have made it possible to extend efficient control, from a given central point, over operations which may be carried on at a great number of widely separated points, and to keep up a close, direct, and intimate action and reaction between the central control and the distributed agents. That means that it has become possible for the organization to be extended in its scope and complexity, and at the same time intensified in its activity. Now whenever such a change in the societal organization becomes possible it also becomes *inevitable,* because there is economy in it. If we confine our attention to industrial undertakings (although states, churches, universities, and other associations and institutions are subject to the same force and sooner or later will have to obey it) we see that the highest degree of organization which is possible is the one that offers the maximum of profit; in it the economic advantage is greatest. There is therefore a gravitation toward this degree of organization. To make an artificial opposition to this tendency from political or alleged moral, or religious, or other motives would be to have no longer any real rule of action; it would amount to submission to the control of warring motives without any real standards or tests.

It is a consequence of the principle just stated that at every point in the history of civilization it has always been necessary to concentrate capital in amounts large relatively to existing facts. In low civilization chiefs control what capital there is, and direct industry; they may be the full owners of all the wealth or only the representatives of a collective theory of ownership. This organization of industry was, at the time, the most efficient, and the tribes which had it prospered better than others. In the classical states with slavery and in the mediæval states with serfdom, the great achievements which realized the utmost that the system was capable of were attained only where wealth was concentrated in productive enterprises in amounts, and under management, which were at the maximum of what the system and the possibilities of the time called for. If we could get rid of some of our notions about liberty and equality, and could lay aside this eighteenth century philosophy according to which human society is to be brought into a state of blessedness, we should get some insight into the might of the societal organization: what it does for us, and what it makes us do. Every day that passes brings us new phenomena of struggle and effort between parts of the societal organization. What do they all mean? They mean that all the individuals and groups are forced against each other in a ceaseless war of interests, by their selfish and mutual efforts to fulfill their career on earth within the conditions set for them by the state of the arts, the facts of the societal organization, and the current dogmas of world philosophy. As each must win his living, or his fortune, or keep his fortune, under these conditions, it is difficult to see what can be meant in the sphere of industrial or economic effort by a "free man." It is no wonder that we so often hear angry outcries about being "slaves" from persons who have had a little experience of the contrast between the current notions and the actual facts.

In fact, what we all need to do is to be taught by the facts in regard to the notions which we ought to adopt, instead of looking at the facts only in order to pass judgment on them and make up our minds how we will change them. If we are willing to be taught by the facts, then the phenomena of the concentration of wealth which we see about us will convince us that they are just what the situation calls for. They ought to be because they are, and because nothing else would serve the interests of society.

I am quite well aware that, in what I have said, I have not met the thoughts and feelings of people who are most troubled about the "concentration of wealth." I have tried to set forth the economic necessity for the concentration of wealth; and I maintain that this is the controlling consideration. Those who care most about the concentration of wealth are indifferent to this consideration; what strikes them most is the fact that there are some rich men. I will, therefore, try to show that this fact also is only another economic justification of the concentration of wealth.

I often see statements published, in which the objectors lay stress upon the great *inequalities* of fortune, and, having set forth the contrast between rich and poor, they rest their case. What law of nature, religion, ethics, or the state is violated by inequalities of fortune? The inequalities prove nothing. Others argue that great fortunes are won by privileges created by law and not by legitimate enterprise and ability. This statement is true, but it is entirely irrelevant; we have to discuss the concentration of wealth within the facts of the institutions, laws, usages, and customs which our ancestors have bequeathed to us and which we allow to stand. If it is proposed to change any of these parts of the societal order, that is a proper subject of discussion, but it is aside from the concentration of wealth. So long as tariffs, patents, etc., are part of the system in which we live, how can it be expected that people will not take advantage of them; what else are they for? As for franchises, a franchise is only an *x* until it has been developed. It never develops itself; it requires capital and skill to develop it. When the enterprise is in the full bloom of prosperity the objectors complain of it, as if the franchise, which never was anything but an empty place where something might be created, had been the completed enterprise. It is interesting to compare the exploitation of the telephone with that of the telegraph fifty years earlier. The latter was, in its day, a far more wonderful invention, but the time and labor required to render it generally available were far greater than what has been required for the telephone, and the fortunes which were won from the former were insignificant in comparison with those which have been won from the latter. Both the public and the promoters acted very differently in the two cases. In these later times promoters seize with avidity upon an enterprise which contains promise, and they push it with energy and ingenuity, while the public is receptive to "improvements"; hence the modern methods offer very great opportunities, and the rewards of those men who can "size up" a situation and develop its controlling elements with sagacity and good judgment, are very great. It is well that they are so, because these rewards stimulate to the utmost all the ambitious and able men, and they make it certain that great and useful inventions will not long remain unexploited as they did formerly. Here comes, then, a new reaction on the economic system; new energy is infused into it, with hope and confidence. We could not spare it and keep up the air of contentment and enthusiastic cheerfulness which characterizes our society. No man can acquire a million without helping a million men to increase their little fortunes all the way down through all the social grades. In some points of view it is an error that we fix our attention so much upon the very rich and overlook the prosperous mass, but the compensating advantage is that the great successes stimulate emulation the most powerfully.

What matters it then that some millionaires are idle, or silly, or vulgar; that their ideas are sometimes futile and their plans grotesque, when they turn aside from money-making? How do they differ in this from any other class? The millionaires are a product of natural selection, acting on the whole body of men to pick out those who can meet the requirement of certain work to be done. In this respect they are just like the great statesmen, or scientific men, or military men. It is because they are thus selected that wealth—both their own and that intrusted to them—aggregates under their hands. Let one of them make a mistake and see how quickly the concentration gives way to dispersion. They may fairly be regarded as the naturally selected agents of society for certain work. They get high wages and live in luxury, but the bargain is a good one for society. There is the intensest competition for their place and occupation. This assures us that all who are competent for this function will be employed in it, so that the cost of it will be reduced to the lowest terms; and furthermore that the competitors will study the proper conduct to be observed in their occupation. This will bring discipline and the correction of arrogance and masterfulness.

X

Who Win by Progress?

In a former article I endeavored to show that the word proletariat, which is now coming into use as a name by which the wages-class is designated by itself and its friends, ought properly to be applied only to persons who live from hand to mouth, who have no definite industrial reliance for support, who have no capital and no reasonable chance of ever getting any, who touch elbows all the time with crime and occasionally fall into its power, and who increase the population through vice. No such class of persons as this exists in modern society, all assertions to the contrary notwithstanding.

Not even in the slums of great modern cities is there any class of persons who could be called proletarians and yet be distinguished from the dangerous and criminal class; for any honest man who finds himself there and is discontented can make his way, by moderate effort, to other places where the conditions are easier.

It is true that a poor man who is fond of the life of a great city cannot secure health, virtue, and capital for his children there at as easy a rate as he could in the country. What then? Shall his fellow-citizens, many of whom have fled to the country, not because they like it but because they can do better for their children in that way, be called upon to enable him to enjoy the delights of the city on the easy terms of the country? It has been asked whether there is not some remedy for the harsh contrasts of wealth and poverty in great cities. There is; it consists in a voluntary disruption of the city and a scattering of its population over the country. Now let us see who will go first—it is safe to predict that among the last to go will be the inhabitants of the slums.

In general, there is no man who is honest and industrious who cannot put himself in a way to maintain himself and his family, misfortune apart, in a condition of substantial comfort. We have any amount of reckless assertion to the contrary; it is asserted that the wages-class is in misery, and suffers from a great number of grievances; but no statement of this kind has ever been made in terms which could be subjected to examination.

It is also asserted that the wages-class have not shared in the advantages of progress. Here it should be noticed, in the first place, that so soon as a member of the non-capitalist class wins capital, he is reckoned with the capitalist class. What we should really need in order to test the question as to what chances the non-capitalists have had for a century past would be a census of the capitalists and non-capitalists a century ago, a similar census now, and a census of those who, in the meantime, have gone over from the latter to the former. The usual method of argument is to show that comparative poverty still exists, and this mode of argument is often extended still further, so that it amounts to arguing that our civilization has accomplished nothing at all because it can be shown that it has not yet got everything done.

In opposition to all this I maintain that the progress of the arts and sciences in the last hundred years has inured most of all to the benefit of the non-capitalists and that the social agitation which we are now witnessing is a proof of the strength, not of the weakness, of that class. If any one wants to see how weak classes have been treated in all ages of the world, let him note how landlords are treated now.

It is a common opinion that the effect of the extension of capital, especially in the form of machinery, is to displace human labor. That opinion is superficial and erroneous; the more complex the tools or machines, the more dependent the owner is on hired help to work them for him. The railroads do not employ fewer men than the canals and stage coaches which they displaced; the sewing machine does not give work to fewer women than the old hand sewing; a new loom calls for more help at another point or the number of new looms is multiplied until they need as much labor as the old ones. All these changes raise the social organization to higher power. We need more men and can support more men, and the machines set free those who are needed to sustain the higher organization by a more refined division of labor. The greater the power of the machines, the greater is the abundance of means of subsistence which the machines produce, and the greater, therefore, is the demand for productive services.

The effect of our progress in the arts and sciences within a century has, therefore, been:

1. That the civilized part of the earth, to say nothing of the other part, is able to support a greater population than ever before; the improvements in transportation have brought within the reach of civilized man vast areas of the earth's surface which were not available a century ago. This fact in itself, for those who can appreciate its significance, is enough to show what class of the population must be chiefly benefited.

2. It has been made cheap and easy for those who had nothing but strong hands and good will to get away from the crowded centers of population to acquire almost without cost land which would richly repay their labor, and to send their products to those markets, however distant, which would return them the largest amount of other products in exchange. Hence the accumulation of capital has outstripped the growth of population, great as the latter has been. It certainly would be a strange social phenomenon if the century which has seen the new continents of America, Australia, and Africa opened to the use of civilized man had also seen the mass of civilized men reduced to lower comfort than they previously enjoyed. The economists and social philosophers who have given countenance to this notion have not only made a professional blunder but also incurred a great responsibility.

3. It is said, however, that the gains have all been won by landlords and capitalists. In truth the vast increase in the production of means of subsistence, won at constantly diminishing outlay

of labor and capital, has lowered money prices and made money wages worth more, and has, at the same time, lowered the rate of interest on capital and increased the demand for labor. It is not at all astonishing that the results have combined and accumulated so as to produce a crisis.

4. It is the fact, also, that the improvements have lowered the pressure of population at the old centers and have, therefore, lowered the rent of land, so that landlords are in the way of being ruined and the old landed aristocracies seem doomed to extinction.

It seems to be believed that we can have all these changes, and that the non-capitalist class can win all the benefit from them without any correlative inconvenience; but that is impossible in the nature of things. The changes which have come about have made life more stringent and exacting for everybody. The rewards of prudence and intelligence are more ample and the penalties of heedlessness and adherence to routine are greater than ever before; every one is forced to "keep up." The more the machines do, the more the rational animal, man, needs to bring brains to bear to rise above the machines. In a sense, our whole society is machine-ridden; it is our fate; it is the price we pay for living in an age of steam, with all the glories of which we boast. The man who has won most of all from the progress is the man who possesses executive power and organizing ability. We get together vast masses of capital and hundreds of laborers, and the happiness or misery of thousands comes to depend on the man whose judgment and knowledge decide what shall be done, and how. We cannot break out of this intense and exacting social organization without sacrificing our means of comfort and throwing thousands into distress; hence we pay the man who can manage the organization a monopoly price for his rare and indispensable abilities.

Next to these, however, who are not capitalists and who are so few that they can hardly be spoken of as a class, the wage-earners have won. They run a greater risk than formerly of interruptions of work and of being compelled to sacrifice routine knowledge which they have acquired. These are weighty risks, and they are weightier in proportion as the organization is more intense, because the higher the organization the harder it is, having once fallen out of it, to get into it again. What the landlords and capitalists will do under the strain which the changes have thrown on them remains to be seen.

The new position of the wage-earner, economically speaking, is the cause of his gain in political power. It is the reason why flatterers and sycophants cluster about him; it is the reason why the laws are warped in his favor, to give him privileges and to force others to yield to him. In our own experience within a year it has been evident that the wage-earners could win their demands when they limited them to a certain measure, that is to say, it has appeared that they were the strong party in the market. They are so, and until the population increases or the land is all taken up they will remain so. As between that which has been achieved and the struggle to achieve, the odds are now largely in favor of the latter.

XI

The New Social Issue

The effect of the great improvements in the arts during the last century is to produce a social and economic order which is controlled by tremendous forces, and which comprehends the whole human race; which is automatic in the mode of its activity; which is delicate and refined in its susceptibility to the influence of interferences. It is therefore at once too vast in its magnitude and scope for us to comprehend it, and too delicate in its operation for us to follow out and master its details.

Under such circumstances the conservative position in social discussion is the only sound position. We do not need to resist all change or discussion—that is not conservatism. We may, however, be sure that the only possible good for society must come of evolution not of revolution. We have a right to condemn, and to refuse our attention to flippant and ignorant criticisms or propositions of reforms; we can rule out at once all plans to reconstruct society, on anybody's system, from the bottom up. We may refuse to act to-day under the motive of redressing some wrong done, ignorantly perhaps, one or two or more centuries ago; or under the motive of bringing in a golden age which we think men can attain to, one or two or more centuries in the future. We may refuse to listen to any propositions which are put forward with menaces and may demand that all who avail themselves of the right of free discussion shall remain upon the field of discussion and refrain from all acts until they have duly and fairly convinced the reason and conscience of the community. We may demand that no strain shall be put on any of our institutions, such as majority rule, by a rash determination to override dissent and remonstrance and to realize something for which there has been collected a hasty majority, animated by heterogeneous motives and purposes.

The institutions which we possess have cost something. Few people seem to know how much—it is one of the great defects in our education that we are not in a position to teach the history of civilization in such a way as to train even educated men to know the cost at which everything which to-day separates us from the brutes has been bought by the generations which have preceded us. As time goes on we can win more, but we shall win it only in the same way, that is, by slow and painful toil and sacrifice, not by adopting some prophet's scheme of the universe; therefore we have a right to ask that all social propositions which demand our attention shall be practical in the best sense, that is, that they shall aim to go forward in the limits and on the lines of sound development out of the past, and that none of our interests shall be put in jeopardy on the chance that Comte, or Spencer, or George, or anybody else has solved the world-problem aright. If anybody has a grievance against the social order, it is, on the simplest principles of common sense, the right of busy men whose attention he demands that he shall set forth in the sharpest and precisest manner what it is; any allegation of injustice which is vague is, by its own tenor, undeserving of attention.

Finally, we each have a right to have our liberty respected in such form as we have inherited it under the laws and institutions of our country. The fashion of the day is to sneer at this demand and to propose to make short work of it so soon as enough power shall have been collected to carry out the projects of certain social sects. Let us, however, give a moment's calm attention to it; the point is worth it, for here is where the tendencies now at work in society are to meet in collision. I do not mean by liberty any power of self-determination which all should allow to each or which each may demand of God, or nature, or society; I mean by it the aggregate of rights, privileges, and prerogatives which the laws and institutions of this country secure to each one of us to-day as conditions under which he may fight out the struggle for existence and the competition of life in this society. I call this liberty a thing which we have a "right" to demand, because, as a fact, the laws give us that right now; when I speak of rights and liberty, therefore, I wish to be understood as standing upon the law of the land and not on any platform of metaphysical or ethical deduction.

Such being the notion of liberty, it is plain that it stands on the line where right and might meet; where war passes over into peace, the guarantees of rights under law taking the place of the domination of might under lawlessness, and the limitation of rights by other rights taking the place of the limitation of powers by other powers. Many of the proposed changes in society aim to alter the demarcation of rights, and they aim to do this, not for a fuller realization of peace, order, liberty, and security, by a nicer adjustment of rights, but they avowedly aim to do it in the interest of certain groups and classes of persons. At this point, therefore, parties must be formed and issues must be joined. On one side is liberty under law, rights and interests being adjusted by the struggle of the parties under the natural laws of the social and industrial order and within barriers set by impersonal and "equal" legislation; on the other, state regulation, consisting of legislation planned to warp rights and interests in favor of selected groups under some *a priori* and arbitrary notion of justice, and administered by persons who, by the fundamental principle of the system, must assume to be competent to decide what ought to be done with us all and who must at the same time themselves be above the most fundamental weaknesses of human nature. There is room for a vast range and variety of opinion and sentiment on either side of this issue, but it is the issue which is upon us and on which every man must take sides.

One of the world-improvers said: "We must know how to do violence to mankind in general, in order to make them happy." He naïvely expressed the sentiment which animates the whole school of opinion to which he belonged, from its extremest right wing to its extremest left wing. They must of course know just what men need to render them happy and they must be fearless in doing violence, that is, in trampling on liberty and causing misery, in order to enforce happiness.

If now we look to see who are to be the victims of the proposed re-adjustment of society, it is plain that they are men who, at this moment, hold the world of trade, industry, finance, transportation, law, and politics in their hands; and they hold it, not because they inherited it or because they belong to any privileged class, but they have obtained control of it by natural selection and because they have made it. Is it likely that they will be intimidated? Are they men to be coerced by clamor, or terrorism, or denunciation, or threats? So far there has scarcely even been discussion except on one side, and the disputants on that side are beginning already to count the battle won. It takes a long time for men who are absorbed in practical life to find out what the literary men are, for the time being, interested in, and still longer for them to make up their minds that talk is to come to anything; that point has not yet been reached, even by the educated community, in regard to the issue which I have described. When it is reached we shall see whether the people of the United States have lost their political sense or not.

It is impossible to look with any complacency on the probability that this issue is to be raised and fought out. No doubt the new power of mankind in these last two or three centuries to reflect on the phenomena and experiences of life has been and is rich in advantage for the race; it has taken the place of an instinctive living under the traditional and simple acquiescence in it, and has developed the reason and conscience of all; but it is at present a sort of disease. A society which brings all its inheritance of thought and faith into question at once, and before it has prepared an adequate apparatus for dealing with the questions and problems which it raises, may fall into chaos. And it is that issue in particular—one which shows that the people are not firm in their conception of liberty and are not ready and hard-headed in their judgment of social fads and whims—which brings with it the greatest jeopardy for the essential welfare of society.

Constitutional liberty, so far as we have been able to realize it, stands just now as a happy phase of civil institutions which we have been able to realize for a moment in the interval between the downfall of aristocracy and the rise of democracy; for there can be no doubt that the epidemic of socialism is only the turning of all social powers in obeisance and flattery toward the new and rising power. We are passing through a transition over to a new illustration of the fact that the thing which forever rules the world is not what is true or what is right, even relatively, but only what is strong. The main question which remains to be solved is whether the elements of strength in the new order are distributed as many now believe; whether democracy is a stable order at all or whether it will at once fall a prey to plutocracy. So surely as democracy yields to socialism, socialism will prove a middle stage toward plutocracy.

XII

The Absurd Effort to Make the World Over

It will not probably be denied that the burden of proof is on
those who affirm that our social condition is utterly diseased and
in need of radical regeneration. My task at present, therefore, is
entirely negative and critical: to examine the allegations of fact
and the doctrines which are put forward to prove the correctness
of the diagnosis and to warrant the use of the remedies proposed.

The propositions put forward by social reformers nowadays
are chiefly of two kinds. There are assertions in historical form,
chiefly in regard to the comparison of existing with earlier social
states, which are plainly based on defective historical knowledge,
or at most on current stock historical dicta which are uncritical
and incorrect. Writers very often assert that something never
existed before because they do not know that it ever existed
before, or that something is worse than ever before because they
are not possessed of detailed information about what has existed
before. The other class of propositions consists of dogmatic statements which, whether true or not, are unverifiable. This class of
propositions is the pest and bane of current economic and social
discussion. Upon a more or less superficial view of some phenomenon a suggestion arises which is embodied in a philosophical
proposition and promulgated as a truth. From the form and
nature of such propositions they can always be brought under
the head of "ethics." This word at least gives them an air of
elevated sentiment and purpose, which is the only warrant they

possess. It is impossible to test or verify them by any investigation or logical process whatsoever. It is therefore very difficult for anyone who feels a high responsibility for historical statements, and who absolutely rejects any statement which is unverifiable, to find a common platform for discussion or to join issue satisfactorily in taking the negative.

When anyone asserts that the class of skilled and unskilled manual laborers of the United States is worse off now in respect to diet, clothing, lodgings, furniture, fuel, and lights; in respect to the age at which they can marry; the number of children they can provide for; the start in life which they can give to their children, and their chances of accumulating capital, than they ever have been at any former time, he makes a reckless assertion for which no facts have been offered in proof. Upon an appeal to facts, the contrary of this assertion would be clearly established. It suffices, therefore, to challenge those who are responsible for the assertion to make it good.

If it is said that the employed class are under much more stringent discipline than they were thirty years ago or earlier, it is true. It is not true that there has been any qualitative change in this respect within thirty years, but it is true that a movement which began at the first settlement of the country has been advancing with constant acceleration and has become a noticeable feature within our time. This movement is the advance in the industrial organization. The first settlement was made by agriculturists, and for a long time there was scarcely any organization. There were scattered farmers, each working for himself, and some small towns with only rudimentary commerce and handicrafts. As the country has filled up, the arts and professions have been differentiated and the industrial organization has been advancing. This fact and its significance has hardly been noticed at all; but the stage of the industrial organization existing at any time, and the rate of advance in its development, are the absolutely controlling social facts. Nine-tenths of the socialistic and semi-socialistic, and sentimental or ethical, suggestions by which we are overwhelmed come from failure to understand the phenomena of the industrial organization and its expansion. It controls us all because we are all in it. It creates the conditions of our existence, sets the limits of our social activity, regulates the bonds of our social relations, determines our conceptions of good and evil, suggests our life-philosophy, molds our inherited political institutions, and reforms the oldest and toughest customs, like marriage and property. I repeat that the turmoil of heterogeneous and antagonistic social whims and speculations in which we live is due to the failure to understand what the industrial organization is and its all-pervading control over human life, while the traditions of our school of philosophy lead us always to approach the industrial organization, not from the side of objective study, but from that of philosophical doctrine. Hence it is that we find that the method of measuring what we see happening by what are called ethical standards, and of proposing to attack the phenomena by methods thence deduced, is so popular.

The advance of a new country from the very simplest social coordination up to the highest organization is a most interesting and instructive chance to study the development of the organization. It has of course been attended all the way along by stricter subordination and higher discipline. All organization implies restriction of liberty. The gain of power is won by narrowing individual range. The methods of business in colonial days were loose and slack to an inconceivable degree. The movement of industry has been all the time toward promptitude, punctuality, and reliability. It has been attended all the way by lamentations about the good old times; about the decline of small industries; about the lost spirit of comradeship between employer and employee; about the narrowing of the interests of the workman; about his conversion into a machine or into a "ware," and about industrial war. These lamentations have all had reference to unquestionable phenomena attendant on advancing organization. In all occupations the same movement is discernible—in the learned professions, in schools, in trade, commerce, and transportation. It is to go on faster than ever, now that the continent is filled up by the first superficial layer of population over its whole extent and the intensification of industry has begun. The great inventions both make the intension of the organization possible and make it inevitable, with all its consequences, whatever they may be. I must expect to be told here, according to the current fashions of thinking, that we ought to control the development of the organization. The first instinct of the modern man is to get a law passed to forbid or prevent what, in his wisdom, he disapproves. A thing which is inevitable, however, is one which we cannot control. We have to make up our minds to it, adjust ourselves to it, and sit down to live with it. Its inevitableness may be disputed, in which case we must re-examine it; but if our analysis is correct, when we reach what is inevitable we reach the end, and our regulations must apply to ourselves, not to the social facts.

Now the intensification of the social organization is what gives us greater social power. It is to it that we owe our increased comfort and abundance. We are none of us ready to sacrifice this. On the contrary, we want more of it. We would not return to the colonial simplicity and the colonial exiguity if we could. If not, then we must pay the price. Our life is bounded on every side by conditions. We can have this if we will agree to submit to that. In the case of industrial power and product the great condition is combination of force under discipline and strict coordination. Hence the wild language about wage-slavery and capitalistic tyranny.

In any state of society no great achievements can be produced without great force. Formerly great force was attainable only by slavery aggregating the power of great numbers of men. Roman civilization was built on this. Ours has been built on steam. It is to be built on electricity. Then we are all forced into an organization around these natural forces and adapted to the methods or their application; and although we indulge in rhetoric about political liberty, nevertheless we find ourselves bound tight in a new set of conditions, which control the modes of our existence and determine the directions in which alone economic and social liberty can go.

If it is said that there are some persons in our time who have become rapidly and in a great degree rich, it is true; if it is said that large aggregations of wealth in the control of individuals is a social danger, it is not true.

The movement of the industrial organization which has just been described has brought out a great demand for men capable of managing great enterprises. Such have been called "captains of industry." The analogy with military leaders suggested by this name is not misleading. The great leaders in the development of the industrial organization need those talents of executive and administrative skill, power to command, courage, and fortitude, which were formerly called for in military affairs and scarcely anywhere else. The industrial army is also as dependent on its captains as a military body is on its generals. One of the worst features of the existing system is that the employees have a constant risk in their employer. If he is not competent to manage the business with success, they suffer with him. Capital also is dependent on the skill of the captain of industry for the certainty and magnitude of its profits. Under these circumstances there has been a great demand for men having the requisite ability for this function. As the organization has advanced, with more impersonal bonds of coherence and wider scope of operations, the value of this functionary has rapidly increased. The possession of the requisite ability is a natural monopoly. Consequently, all the conditions have concurred to give to those who possessed this monopoly excessive and constantly advancing rates of remuneration.

Another social function of the first importance in an intense organization is the solution of those crises in the operation of it which are called the conjuncture of the market. It is through the market that the lines of relation run which preserve the system in harmonious and rhythmical operation. The conjuncture is the momentary sharper misadjustment of supply and demand which indicates that a redistribution of productive effort is called for. The industrial organization needs to be insured against these conjunctures, which, if neglected, produce a crisis and catastrophe; and it needs that they shall be anticipated and guarded against as far as skill and foresight can do it. The rewards of this function for the bankers and capitalists who perform it are very great. The captains of industry and the capitalists who operate on the conjuncture, therefore, if they are successful, win, in these days, great fortunes in a short time. There are no earnings which are more legitimate or for which greater services are rendered to the whole industrial body. The popular notions about this matter really assume that all the wealth accumulated by these classes of persons would be here just the same if they had not existed. They are supposed to have appropriated it out of the common stock. This is so far from being true that, on the contrary, their own wealth would not be but for themselves; and besides that, millions more of wealth, many-fold greater than their own, scattered in the hands of thousands, would not exist but for them.

Within the last two years I have traveled from end to end of the German Empire several times on all kinds of trains. I reached the conviction, looking at the matter from the passenger's standpoint, that, if the Germans could find a Vanderbilt and put their railroads in his hands for twenty-five years, letting him reorganize the system and make twenty-five million dollars out of it for himself in that period, they would make an excellent bargain.

But it is repeated until it has become a commonplace which people are afraid to question, that there is some social danger in the possession of large amounts of wealth by individuals. I ask, Why? I heard a lecture two years ago by a man who holds perhaps the first chair of political economy in the world. He said, among other things, that there was great danger in our day from great accumulations; that this danger ought to be met by taxation, and he referred to the fortune of the Rothschilds and to the great fortunes made in America to prove his point. He omitted, however, to state in what the danger consisted or to specify what harm has ever been done by the Rothschild fortunes or by the great fortunes accumulated in America. It seemed to me that the assertions he was making, and the measures he was recommending, ex-cathedra, were very serious to be thrown out so recklessly. It is hardly to be expected that novelists, popular magazinists, amateur economists, and politicians will be more responsible. It would be easy, however, to show what good is done by accumulations of capital in a few hands—that is, under close and direct management, permitting prompt and accurate application; also to tell what harm is done by loose and unfounded denunciations of any social component or any social group. In the recent debates on the income tax the assumption that great accumulations of wealth are socially harmful and ought to be broken down by taxation was treated as an axiom, and we had direct proof how dangerous it is to fit out the average politician with such unverified and unverifiable dogmas as his warrant for his modes of handling the direful tool of taxation.

Great figures are set out as to the magnitude of certain fortunes and the proportionate amount of the national wealth held by a fraction of the population, and eloquent exclamation-points are set against them. If the figures were beyond criticism, what would they prove? Where is the rich man who is oppressing anybody? If there was one, the newspapers would ring with it. The facts about the accumulation of wealth do not constitute a plutocracy, as I will show below. Wealth, in itself considered, is only power, like steam, or electricity, or knowledge. The question of its good or ill turns on the question how it will be used. To prove any harm in aggregations of wealth it must be shown that great wealth is, as a rule, in the ordinary course of social affairs, put to a mischievous use. This cannot be shown beyond the very slightest degree, if at all.

Therefore, all the allegations of general mischief, social corruption, wrong, and evil in our society must be referred back to those who make them for particulars and specifications. As they are offered to us we cannot allow them to stand, because we discern in them faulty observation of facts, or incorrect interpretation of facts, or a construction of facts according to some philosophy, or misunderstanding of phenomena and their relations, or incorrect inferences, or crooked deductions.

Assuming, however, that the charges against the existing "capitalistic"—that is, industrial—order of things are established, it is proposed to remedy the ill by reconstructing the industrial system on the principles of democracy. Once more we must untangle the snarl of half ideas and muddled facts.

Democracy is, of course, a word to conjure with. We have a democratic-republican political system, and we like it so well that we are prone to take any new step which can be recommended as "democratic" or which will round out some "principle" of democracy to a fuller fulfillment. Everything connected with this domain of political thought is crusted over with false historical traditions, cheap philosophy, and undefined terms, but it is useless to try to criticize it. The whole drift of the world for five hundred years has been toward democracy. That drift, produced by great discoveries and inventions, and by the discovery of a new continent, has raised the middle class out of the servile class. In alliance with the crown they crushed the feudal classes. They made the crown absolute in order to do it. Then they turned against the crown and, with the aid of the handicraftsmen and peasants, conquered it. Now the next conflict which must inevitably come is that between the middle capitalist class and the proletariat, as the word has come to be used. If a certain construction is put on this conflict, it may be called that between democracy and plutocracy, for it seems that industrialism must be developed into plutocracy by the conflict itself. That is the conflict which stands before civilized society to-day. All the signs of the times indicate its commencement, and it is big with fate to mankind and to civilization.

Although we cannot criticise democracy profitably, it may be said of it, with reference to our present subject, that up to this time democracy never has done anything, either in politics, social affairs, or industry, to prove its power to bless mankind. If we confine our attention to the United States, there are three difficulties with regard to its alleged achievements, and they all have the most serious bearing on the proposed democratization of industry.

1. The time during which democracy has been tried in the United States is too short to warrant any inferences. A century or two is a very short time in the life of political institutions, and if the circumstances change rapidly during the period the experiment is vitiated.

2. The greatest question of all about American democracy is whether it is a cause or a consequence. It is popularly assumed to be a cause, and we ascribe to its beneficent action all the political vitality, all the easiness of social relations, all the industrial activity and enterprise which we experience and which we value and enjoy. I submit, however, that, on a more thorough examination of the matter, we shall find that democracy is a consequence. There are economic and sociological causes for our political vitality and vigor, for the ease and elasticity of our social relations, and for our industrial power and success. Those causes have also produced democracy, given it success, and have made its faults and errors innocuous. Indeed, in any true philosophy,

it must be held that in the economic forces which control the material prosperity of a population lie the real causes of its political institutions, its social class-adjustments, its industrial prosperity, its moral code, and its world-philosophy. If democracy and the industrial system are both products of the economic conditions which exist, it is plainly absurd to set democracy to defeat those conditions in the control of industry. If, however, it is not true that democracy is a consequence, and I am well aware that very few people believe it, then we must go back to the view that democracy is a cause. That being so, it is difficult to see how democracy, which has had a clear field here in America, is not responsible for the ills which Mr. Bellamy[1] and his comrades in opinion see in our present social state, and it is difficult to see the grounds of asking us to intrust it also with industry. The first and chief proof of success of political measures and systems is that, under them, society advances in health and vigor and that industry develops without causing social disease. If this has not been the case in America, American democracy has not succeeded. Neither is it easy to see how the masses, if they have undertaken to rule, can escape the responsibilities of ruling, especially so far as the consequences affect themselves. If, then, they have brought all this distress upon themselves under the present system, what becomes of the argument for extending the system to a direct and complete control of industry?

3. It is by no means certain that democracy in the United States has not, up to this time, been living on a capital inherited from aristocracy and industrialism. We have no pure democracy. Our democracy is limited at every turn by institutions which were developed in England in connection with industrialism and aristocracy, and these institutions are of the essence of our system. While our people are passionately democratic in temper and will not tolerate a doctrine that one man is not as good as another, they have common sense enough to know that he is not; and it seems that they love and cling to the conservative institutions quite as strongly as they do to the democratic philosophy. They

[1] Edward Bellamy (1850-1898) wrote the immensely popular utopian socialist novel, *Looking Backward,* which was published in 1888. [S.P.]

are, therefore, ruled by men who talk philosophy and govern by
the institutions. Now it is open to Mr. Bellamy to say that the
reason why democracy in America seems to be open to the charge
made in the last paragraph, of responsibility for all the ill which
he now finds in our society, is because it has been infected with
industrialism (capitalism); but in that case he must widen the
scope of his proposition and undertake to purify democracy before turning industry over to it. The socialists generally seem to
think that they make their undertakings easier when they widen
their scope, and make them easiest when they propose to remake
everything; but in truth social tasks increase in difficulty in an
enormous ratio as they are widened in scope.

The question, therefore, arises, if it is proposed to reorganize
the social system on the principles of American democracy,
whether the institutions of industrialism are to be retained.
If so, all the virus of capitalism will be retained. It is forgotten,
in many schemes of social reformation in which it is proposed to
mix what we like with what we do not like, in order to extirpate
the latter, that each must undergo a reaction from the other, and
that what we like may be extirpated by what we do not like. We
may find that instead of democratizing capitalism we have capi-
talized democracy—that is, have brought in plutocracy. Plutocracy
is a political system in which the ruling force is wealth. The
denunciation of capital which we hear from all the reformers is
the most eloquent proof that the greatest power in the world
to-day is capital. They know that it is, and confess it most when
they deny it most strenuously. At present the power of capital is
social and industrial, and only in a small degree political. So far
as capital is political, it is on account of political abuses, such
as tariffs and special legislation on the one hand and legislative
strikes on the other. These conditions exist in the democracy to
which it is proposed to transfer the industries. What does that
mean except bringing all the power of capital once for all into
the political arena and precipitating the conflict of democracy
and plutocracy at once? Can anyone imagine that the masterfulness, the overbearing disposition, the greed of gain, and the ruthlessness in methods, which are the faults of the master of industry

at his worst, would cease when he was a functionary of the State, which had relieved him of risk and endowed him with authority? Can anyone imagine that politicians would no longer be corruptly fond of money, intriguing, and crafty when they were charged, not only with patronage and government contracts, but also with factories, stores, ships, and railroads? Could we expect anything except that, when the politician and the master of industry were joined in one, we should have the vices of both unchecked by the restraints of either? In any socialistic state there will be one set of positions which will offer chances of wealth beyond the wildest dreams of avarice; viz., on the governing committees. Then there will be rich men whose wealth will indeed be a menace to social interests, and instead of industrial peace there will be such war as no one has dreamed of yet: the war between the political ins and outs—that is, between those who are on the committee and those who want to get on it.

We must not drop the subject of democracy without one word more. The Greeks already had occasion to notice a most serious distinction between two principles of democracy which lie at its roots. Plutarch says that Solon got the archonship in part by promising equality, which some understood of esteem and dignity, others of measure and number. There is one democratic principle which means that each man should be esteemed for his merit and worth, for just what he is, without regard to birth, wealth, rank, or other adventitious circumstances. The other principle is that each one of us ought to be equal to all the others in what he gets and enjoys. The first principle is only partially realizable, but, so far as it goes, it is elevating and socially progressive and profitable. The second is not capable of an intelligible statement. The first is a principle of industrialism. It proceeds from and is intelligible only in a society built on the industrial virtues, free endeavor, security of property, and repression of the baser vices; that is, in a society whose industrial system is built on labor and exchange. The other is only a rule of division for robbers who have to divide plunder or monks who have to divide gifts. If, therefore, we want to democratize industry in the sense of the first principle, we need only perfect what we have now, especially

on its political side. If we try to democratize it in the sense of
the other principle, we corrupt politics at one stroke; we enter
upon an industrial enterprise which will waste capital and bring
us all to poverty, and we set loose greed and envy as ruling social
passions.

If this poor old world is as bad as they say, one more reflection
may check the zeal of the headlong reformer. It is at any rate a
tough old world. It has taken its trend and curvature and all its
twists and tangles from a long course of formation. All its wry
and crooked gnarls and knobs are therefore stiff and stubborn.
If we puny men by our arts can do anything at all to straighten
them, it will only be by modifying the tendencies of some of the
forces at work, so that, after a sufficient time, their action may
be changed a little and slowly the lines of movement may be
modified. This effort, however, can at most be only slight, and
it will take a long time. In the meantime spontaneous forces will
be at work, compared with which our efforts are like those of a
man trying to deflect a river, and these forces will have changed
the whole problem before our interferences have time to make
themselves felt. The great stream of time and earthly things will
sweep on just the same in spite of us. It bears with it now all the
errors and follies of the past, the wreckage of all the philosophies,
the fragments of all the civilizations, the wisdom of all the abandoned ethical systems, the debris of all the institutions, and the
penalties of all the mistakes. It is only in imagination that we
stand by and look at and criticize it and plan to change it. Everyone of us is a child of his age and cannot get out of it. He is in
the stream and is swept along with it. All his sciences and philosophy come to him out of it. Therefore the tide will not be
changed by us. It will swallow up both us and our experiments.
It will absorb the efforts at change and take them into itself as
new but trivial components, and the great movement of tradition
and work will go on unchanged by our fads and schemes. The
things which will change it are the great discoveries and inventions, the new reactions inside the social organism, and the
changes in the earth itself on account of changes in the cosmical
forces. These causes will make of it just what, in fidelity to them,

it ought to be. The men will be carried along with it and be made by it. The utmost they can do by their cleverness will be to note and record their course as they are carried along, which is what we do now, and is that which leads us to the vain fancy that we can make or guide the movement. That is why it is the greatest folly of which a man can be capable, to sit down with a slate and pencil to plan out a new social world.

Classics in History Series

* Also available in a limited clothbound edition